Charles Alexander Eastman
(Ohiyesa)

FROM THE DEEP WOODS TO CIVILIZATION

CHARLES ALEXANDER EASTMAN
(OHIYESA)

DOVER PUBLICATIONS, INC.
Mineola, New York

Bibliographical Note

This Dover edition, first published in 2003, is an unabridged republication of the work originally published by Little, Brown, and Company, Boston, 1916. For this edition the text has been reset and the illustrations relocated as near as possible to their original position in the book.

Library of Congress Cataloging-in-Publication Data

Eastman, Charles Alexander, 1858–1939.
    From the deep woods to civilization / Charles Alexander Eastman (Ohiyesa).
       p. cm.
    Originally published: Boston : Little, Brown, 1916.
    Includes index.
    ISBN-13: 978-0-486-43088-1 (pbk.)
    ISBN-10: 0-486-43088-X (pbk.)
    1. Eastman, Charles Alexander, 1858–1939. 2. Santee Indians—Biography.
I. Title.

E99.S22E183 2003
973.04'9752—dc21
[B]

            2003048930

Manufactured in the United States by LSC Communications
43088X09   2017
www.doverpublications.com

Foreword

"INDIAN BOYHOOD," published first in 1902 and in many subsequent editions, pictures the first of three distinct periods in the life of the writer of this book. His childhood and youth were a part of the free wilderness life of the first American—a life that is gone forever! By dint of much persuasion, the story has now been carried on from the point of that plunge into the unknown with which the first book ends, a change so abrupt and so overwhelming that the boy of fifteen "felt as if he were dead and travelling to the spirit land." We are now to hear of a single-hearted quest throughout eighteen years of adolescence and early maturity, for the attainment of the modern ideal of Christian culture: and again of a quarter of a century devoted to testing that hard-won standard in various fields of endeavor, partly by holding it up before his own race, and partly by interpreting their racial ideals to the white man, leading in the end to a partial reaction in favor of the earlier, the simpler, perhaps the more spiritual philosophy. It is clearly impossible to tell the whole story, but much that cannot be told may be read "between the lines." The broad outlines, the salient features of an uncommon experience are here set forth in the hope that they may strengthen for some readers the conception of our common humanity.

E. G. E.

Contents

List of Illustrations

ix

FROM THE DEEP WOODS
TO CIVILIZATION

I. The Way Opens

One can never be sure of what a day may bring to pass. At the age of fifteen years, the deepening current of my life swung upon such a pivotal day, and in the twinkling of an eye its whole course was utterly changed; as if a little mountain brook should pause and turn upon itself to gather strength for the long journey toward an unknown ocean.

From childhood I was consciously trained to be a man; that was, after all, the basic thing; but after this I was trained to be a warrior and a hunter, and not to care for money or possessions, but to be in the broadest sense a public servant. After arriving at a reverent sense of the pervading presence of the Spirit and Giver of Life, and a deep consciousness of the brotherhood of man, the first thing for me to accomplish was to adapt myself perfectly to natural things—in other words, to harmonize myself with nature. To this end I was made to build a body both symmetrical and enduring—a house for the soul to live in—a sturdy house, defying the elements. I must have faith and patience; I must learn self-control and be able to maintain silence. I must do with as little as possible and start with nothing most of the time, because a true Indian always shares whatever he may possess.

I felt no hatred for our tribal foes. I looked upon them more as the college athlete regards his rivals from another college. There was no thought of destroying a nation, taking away their country or reducing the people to servitude, for my race rather

1

honored and bestowed gifts upon their enemies at the next peaceful meeting, until they had adopted the usages of the white man's warfare for spoliation and conquest.

There was one unfortunate thing about my early training, however; that is, I was taught never to spare a citizen of the United States, although we were on friendly terms with the Canadian white men. The explanation is simple. My people had been turned out of some of the finest country in the world, now forming the great states of Minnesota and Iowa. The Americans pretended to buy the land at ten cents an acre, but never paid the price; the debt stands unpaid to this day. Because they did not pay, the Sioux protested; finally came the outbreak of 1862 in Minnesota, when many settlers were killed, and forthwith our people, such as were left alive, were driven by the troops into exile.

My father, who was among the fugitives in Canada, had been betrayed by a half-breed across the United States line, near what is now the city of Winnipeg. Some of the party were hanged at Fort Snelling, near St. Paul. We supposed, and, in fact, we were informed that all were hanged. This was why my uncle, in whose family I lived, had taught me never to spare a white man from the United States.

During the summer and winter of 1871, the band of Sioux to which I belonged—a clan of the Wah´petons, or "Dwellers among the Leaves"—roamed in the upper Missouri region and along the Yellowstone River. In that year I tasted to the full the joy and plenty of wild existence. I saw buffalo, elk, and antelope in herds numbering thousands. The forests teemed with deer, and in the "Bad Lands" dwelt the Big Horns or Rocky Mountain sheep. At this period, grizzly bears were numerous and were brought into camp quite commonly, like any other game.

We frequently met and camped with the Hudson Bay half-breeds in their summer hunt of the buffalo, and we were on terms of friendship with the Assiniboines and the Crees, but in frequent collision with the Blackfeet, the Gros Ventres, and the Crows. However, there were times of truce when all met in peace for a great midsummer festival and exchange of gifts. The Sioux roamed over an area nearly a thousand miles in extent. In the summer we gathered together in large numbers, but towards fall we would divide into small groups or bands and scatter for the trapping and the winter hunt. Most of us hugged the wooded river bottoms; some depended entirely upon the buffalo for food, while others, and among these my immediate kindred, hunted all kinds of game, and trapped and fished as well.

Thus I was trained thoroughly for an all-round out-door life and for all natural emergencies. I was a good rider and a good shot with the bow and arrow, alert and alive to everything that came within my ken. I had never known nor ever expected to know any life but this.

In the winter and summer of 1872, we drifted toward the southern part of what is now Manitoba. In this wild, rolling country I rapidly matured, and laid, as I supposed, the foundations of my life career, never dreaming of anything beyond this manful and honest, unhampered existence. My horse and my dog were my closest companions. I regarded them as brothers, and if there was a hereafter, I expected to meet them there. With them I went out daily into the wilderness to seek inspiration and store up strength for coming manhood. My teachers dreamed no more than I of any change in my prospects. I had now taken part in all our tribal activities except that of war, and was nearly old enough to be initiated into the ritual of the war-path. The world was full of natural rivalry; I was eager for the day.

I had attained the age of fifteen years and was about to enter into and realize a man's life, as we Indians understood it, when the change came. One fine September morning as I returned from the daily hunt, there seemed to be an unusual stir and excitement as I approached our camp. My faithful grandmother was on the watch and met me to break the news. "Your father has come—he whom we thought dead at the hands of the white men," she said.

It was a day of miracle in the deep Canadian wilderness, before the Canadian Pacific had been even dreamed of, while the Indian and the buffalo still held sway over the vast plains of Manitoba east of the Rocky Mountains. It was, perhaps, because

Many Lightnings. English Name, Jacob Eastman.
From an Old Daguerreotype of Dr. Eastman's Father.

he was my honored father that I lent my bewildered ear to his eloquent exposition of the so-called civilized life, or the way of the white man. I could not doubt my own father, so mysteriously come back to us, as it were, from the spirit land; yet there was a voice within saying to me, "A false life! a treacherous life!"

In accordance with my training, I asked few questions, although many arose in my mind. I simply tried silently to fit the new ideas like so many blocks into the pattern of my philosophy, while according to my untutored logic some did not seem to have straight sides or square corners to fit in with the cardinal principles of eternal justice. My father had been converted by Protestant missionaries, and he gave me a totally new vision of the white man, as a religious man and a kindly. But when he related how he had set apart every seventh day for religious duties and the worship of God, laying aside every other occupation on that day, I could not forbear exclaiming, "Father! and does he then forget God during the six days and do as he pleases?"

"Our own life, I will admit, is the best in a world of our own, such as we have enjoyed for ages," said my father. "But here is a race which has learned to weigh and measure everything, time and labor and the results of labor, and has learned to accumulate and preserve both wealth and the records of experience for future generations. You yourselves know and use some of the wonderful inventions of the white man, such as guns and gunpowder, knives and hatchets, garments of every description, and there are thousands of other things both beautiful and useful.

"Above all, they have their Great Teacher, whom they call Jesus, and he taught them to pass on their wisdom and knowledge to all other races. It is true that they have subdued and taught many peoples, and our own must eventually bow to this law; the sooner we accept their mode of life and follow their teaching, the better it will be for us all. I have thought much on this matter and such is my conclusion."

There was a mingling of admiration and indignation in my mind as I listened. My father's two brothers were still far from being convinced; but filial duty and affection overweighed all my prejudices. I was bound to go back with him as he desired me to do, and my grandmother and her only daughter accompanied us on the perilous journey.

The line between Canada and the United States was closely watched at this time by hostile Indians, therefore my father thought it best to make a dash for Devil's Lake, in North Dakota, where he could get assistance if necessary. He knew Major Forbes, who was in command of the military post and the agency. Our guide we knew to be an unscrupulous man, who could easily betray us for a kettle of whisky or a pony. One of the first things I observed was my father's reading aloud from a book every morning and evening, followed by a very strange song and a prayer. Although all he said was in Indian, I did not understand it fully. He apparently talked aloud to the "Great Mystery," asking for our safe guidance back to his home in the States. The first reading of this book of which I have any recollection was the twenty-third Psalm, and the first hymn he sang in my presence was to the old tune of Ortonville. It was his Christian faith and devotion which was perhaps the strongest influence toward my change of heart and complete change of my purpose in life.

I think it was at our second encampment that we met a large caravan of Canadian half-breeds accompanied by a band of Northern Ojibways. As was usual with the former, they had plenty of whisky. They were friendly enough with us, at least while sober, but the Indians were not. Father showed them his papers as a United States citizen and a letter from Major Forbes, telling of his peaceful mission, but we could not trust our ancestral enemies, the Ojibways, especially when excited with strong drink. My father was calm and diplomatic throughout, but thus privately instructed me:

"My son, conceal yourself in the woods; and if the worst comes you must flee on your swift pony. Before daylight you can pass the deep woods and cross the Assiniboine River." He handed me a letter to Major Forbes. I said, "I will try," and as soon as it was dark, I hid myself, to be in readiness. Meanwhile, my father called the leading half-breeds together and told them again that he was under the protection of his government, also that the Sioux would hold them responsible if anything happened to us. Just then they discovered that another young brave and I were not to be found, which made them think that father had dispatched us to the nearest military post for help. They immediately led away their drunken comrades and made a big talk to their Ojibway friends, so that we remained undisturbed until morning.

Some days later, at the south end of Devil's Lake, I left our camp early to shoot some ducks when the morning flight should begin. Suddenly, when out of sight of the others, my eye caught a slight movement in the rank grass. Instinctively I dropped and flattened myself upon the ground, but soon a quick glance behind me showed plainly the head of a brave hidden behind a bush. I waited, trying to figure out some plan of escape, yet facing the probability that I was already surrounded, until I caught sight of another head almost in front and still another to my left.

In the moments that elapsed after I fully realized my situation, I thought of almost everything that had happened to me up to that day; of a remarkable escape from the Ojibways, of the wild pets I had had, and of my playmates in the Canadian camps whom I should never see again. I also thought with more curiosity than fear of the "Great Mystery" that I was so soon to enter. As these thoughts were passing through my mind, I carelessly moved and showed myself plainly to the enemy.

Suddenly, from behind the nearest bush, came the sound of my own Sioux tongue and the words, "Are you a Sioux?" Possibly my countenance may not have changed much, but certainly I grew weak with surprise and relief. As soon as I answered "Yes!" I was surrounded by a group of warriors of my tribe, who chuckled at the joke that had come so near to costing me my life, for one of them explained that he had been on the point of firing when I exposed myself so plainly that he saw I was not an Ojibway in war paint but probably a Sioux like himself.

After a variety of adventures, we arrived at the canvas city of Jamestown, then the terminal point of the Northern Pacific railroad. I was out watering the ponies when a terrific peal of thunder burst from a spotless blue sky, and indeed seemed to me to be running along the surface of the ground. The terrified ponies instantly stampeded, and I confess I was not far behind them, when a monster with one fiery eye poked his head around a corner of the hill. When we reached camp, my father kindly explained, and I was greatly relieved.

It was a peaceful Indian summer day when we reached Flandreau, in Dakota Territory, the citizen Indian settlement, and found the whole community gathered together to congratulate and welcome us home.

II. My First School Days

It was less than a month since I had been a rover and a hunter in the Manitoba wilderness, with no thoughts save those which concern the most free and natural life of an Indian. Now, I found myself standing near a rude log cabin on the edge of a narrow strip of timber, overlooking the fertile basin of the Big Sioux River. As I gazed over the rolling prairie land, all I could see was that it met the sky at the horizon line. It seemed to me vast and vague and endless, as was my conception of the new trail which I had taken and my dream of the far-off goal.

My father's farm of 160 acres, which he had taken up and improved under the United States homestead laws, lay along the north bank of the river. The nearest neighbor lived a mile away, and all had flourishing fields of wheat, Indian corn and potatoes. Some two miles distant, where the Big Sioux doubled upon itself in a swinging loop, rose the mission church and schoolhouse, the only frame building within forty miles.

Our herd of ponies was loose upon the prairie, and it was my first task each morning to bring them into the log corral. On this particular morning I lingered, finding some of them, like myself, who loved their freedom too well and would not come in.

The man who had built the cabin—it was his first house, and therefore he was proud of it—was tall and manly looking. He stood in front of his pioneer home with a resolute face.

He had been accustomed to the buffalo-skin teepee all his life, until he opposed the white man and was defeated and made a prisoner of war at Davenport, Iowa. It was because of his meditations during those four years in a military prison that he had

9

severed himself from his tribe and taken up a homestead. He declared that he would never join in another Indian outbreak, but would work with his hands for the rest of his life.

"I have hunted every day," he said, "for the support of my family. I sometimes chase the deer all day. One must work, and work hard, whether chasing the deer or planting corn. After all, the corn-planting is the surer provision."

These were my father's new views, and in this radical change of life he had persuaded a few other families to join him. They formed a little colony at Flandreau, on the Big Sioux River.

To be sure, his beginnings in civilization had not been attended with all the success that he had hoped for. One year the crops had been devoured by grasshoppers, and another year ruined by drought. But he was still satisfied that there was no alternative for the Indian. He was now anxious to have his boys learn the English language and something about books, for he could see that these were the "bow and arrows" of the white man.

"O-hee-ye-sa!" called my father, and I obeyed the call. "It is time for you to go to school, my son," he said, with his usual air of decision. We had spoken of the matter more than once, yet it seemed hard when it came to the actual undertaking.

I remember quite well how I felt as I stood there with eyes fixed upon the ground.

"And what am I to do at the school?" I asked finally, with much embarrassment.

"You will be taught the language of the white man, and also how to count your money and tell the prices of your horses and of your furs. The white teacher will first teach you the signs by which you can make out the words on their books. They call them A, B, C, and so forth. Old as I am, I have learned some of them."

The matter having been thus far explained, I was soon on my way to the little mission school, two miles distant over the prairie. There was no clear idea in my mind as to what I had to do, but as I galloped along the road I turned over and over what my father had said, and the more I thought of it the less I was satisfied. Finally I said aloud:

"Why do we need a sign language, when we can both hear and

Typical Indian Log Cabin, such as Dr. Eastman's Father
lived in at Flandreau, Dakota Territory.

At Home in the Wilderness. A Group of Indian Teepees.

talk?" And unconsciously I pulled on the lariat and the pony came to a stop. I suppose I was half curious and half in dread about this "learning white men's ways." Meanwhile the pony had begun to graze.

While thus absorbed in thought, I was suddenly startled by the yells of two other Indian boys and the noise of their ponies' hoofs. I pulled the pony's head up just as the two strangers also pulled up and stopped their panting ponies at my side. They stared at me for a minute, while I looked at them out of the corners of my eyes.

"Where are you going? Are you going to our school?" volunteered one of the boys at last.

To this I replied timidly: "My father told me to go to a place where the white men's ways are taught, and to learn the sign language."

"That's good—we are going there too! Come on, Red Feather, let's try another race! I think, if we had not stopped, my pony would have outrun yours. Will you race with us?" he continued, addressing me; and we all started our ponies at full speed.

I soon saw that the two strange boys were riding erect and soldier-like. "That must be because they have been taught to be like the white man," I thought. I allowed my pony a free start and leaned forward until the animal drew deep breaths, then I slid back and laid my head against the pony's shoulder, at the same time raising my quirt, and he leaped forward with a will! I yelled as I passed the other boys, and pulled up when I reached the crossing. The others stopped, too, and surveyed pony and river from head to foot, as if they had never seen us before.

"You have a fast pony. Did you bring him back with you from Canada?" Red Feather asked. "I think you are the son of Many Lightnings, whom he brought home the other day," the boy added.

"Yes, this is my own pony. My uncle in Canada always used him to chase the buffalo, and he has ridden him in many battles." I spoke with considerable pride.

"Well, as there are no more buffalo to chase now, your pony will have to pull the plow like the rest. But if you ride him to school, you can join in the races. On the holy days the young men race horses, too." Red Feather and White Fish spoke both together, while I listened attentively, for everything was strange to me.

"What do you mean by the 'holy days'?" I asked.

"Well, that's another of the white people's customs. Every seventh day they call a 'holy day,' and on that day they go to a 'Holy House,' where they pray to their Great Mystery. They also say that no one should work on that day."

This definition of Sunday and church-going set me to thinking again, for I never knew before that there was any difference in the days.

"But how do you count the days, and how do you know what day to begin with?" I inquired.

"Oh, that's easy! The white men have everything in their books. They know how many days in a year, and they have even divided the day itself into so many equal parts; in fact, they have divided them again and again until they know how many times one can breathe in a day," said White Fish, with the air of a learned man.

"That's impossible," I thought, so I shook my head.

By this time we had reached the second crossing of the river, on whose bank stood the little mission school. Thirty or forty Indian children stood about, curiously watching the newcomer as we came up the steep bank. I realized for the first time that I was an object of curiosity, and it was not a pleasant feeling. On the other hand, I was considerably interested in the strange appearance of these school-children.

They all had on some apology for white man's clothing, but their pantaloons belonged neither to the order *short* nor to the *long*. Their coats, some of them, met only half-way by the help of long strings. Others were lapped over in front, and held on by a string of some sort fastened round the body. Some of their hats were brimless and others without crowns, while most were fantastically painted. The hair of all the boys was cut short, and, in spite of the evidences of great effort to keep it down, it stood erect like porcupine quills. I thought, as I stood on one side and took a careful observation of the motley gathering, that if I had to look like these boys in order to obtain something of the white man's learning, it was time for me to rebel.

The boys played ball and various other games, but I tied my pony to a tree and then walked up to the schoolhouse and stood there as still as if I had been glued to the wall. Presently the teacher came out and rang a bell, and all the children went in, but I waited for some time before entering, and then slid inside and took the seat nearest the door. I felt singularly out of place, and for the twentieth time wished my father had not sent me.

When the teacher spoke to me, I had not the slightest idea what he meant, so I did not trouble myself to make any demonstration, for fear of giving offense. Finally he asked in broken Sioux: "What is your name?" Evidently he had not been among the Indians long, or he would not have asked that question. It takes a tactician and a diplomat to get an Indian to tell his name! The poor man was compelled to give up the attempt and resume his seat on the platform.

He then gave some unintelligible directions, and, to my great surprise, the pupils in turn held their books open and talked the talk of a strange people. Afterward the teacher made some curious signs upon a blackboard on the wall, and seemed to ask the children to read them. To me they did not compare in interest with my bird's-track and fish-fin studies on the sands. I was something like a wild cub caught overnight, and appearing in the corral next morning with the lambs. I had seen nothing thus far to prove to me the good of civilization.

Meanwhile the children grew more familiar, and whispered references were made to the "new boy's" personal appearance. At last he was called "Baby" by one of the big boys; but this was not meant for him to hear, so he did not care to hear. He rose silently and walked out. He did not dare to do or say anything in departing. The boys watched him as he led his pony to the river to drink and then jumped upon his back and started for home at a good pace. They cheered as he started over the hills: "Hoo-oo! hoo-oo! there goes the long-haired boy!"

When I was well out of sight of the school, I pulled in my pony and made him walk slowly home.

"Will going to that place make a man brave and strong?" I asked myself. "I must tell my father that I cannot stay here. I must go back to my uncle in Canada, who taught me to hunt and shoot and to be a brave man. They might as well try to make a buffalo build houses like a beaver as to teach me to be a white man," I thought.

It was growing late when at last I appeared at the cabin. "Why, what is the matter?" quoth my old grandmother, who had taken especial pride in me as a promising young hunter. Really, my face had assumed a look of distress and mental pressure that frightened the superstitious old woman. She held her peace, however, until my father returned.

"Ah," she said then, "I never fully believed in these new manners! The Great Mystery cannot make a mistake. I say it is against our religion to change the customs that have been practiced by our people ages back—so far back that no one can remember it. Many of the school-children have died, you have told me. It is not strange. You have offended Him, because you have made these children change the ways he has given us. I must know more about this matter before I give my consent." Grandmother had opened her mind in unmistakable terms, and the whole family was listening to her in silence.

Then my hard-headed father broke the pause. "Here is one Sioux who will sacrifice everything to win the wisdom of the white man! We have now entered upon this life, and there is no going back. Besides, one would be like a hobbled pony without learning to live like those among whom we must live."

During father's speech my eyes had been fixed upon the burning logs that stood on end in the huge mud chimney in a corner of the cabin. I didn't want to go to that place again; but father's logic was too strong for me, and the next morning I had my long hair cut, and started in to school in earnest.

I obeyed my father's wishes, and went regularly to the little day-school, but as yet my mind was in darkness. What has all this talk of books to do with hunting, or even with planting corn? I thought. The subject occupied my thoughts more and more, doubtless owing to my father's decided position on the matter; while, on the other hand, my grandmother's view of this new life was not encouraging.

I took the situation seriously enough, and I remember I went with it where all my people go when they want light—into the thick woods. I needed counsel, and human counsel did not satisfy me. I had been taught to seek the "Great Mystery" in silence, in the deep forest or on the height of the mountain. There were no mountains here, so I retired into the woods. I knew nothing of the white man's religion; I only followed the teaching of my ancestors.

When I came back, my heart was strong. I desired to follow the new trail to the end. I knew that, like the little brook, it must lead to larger and larger ones until it became a resistless river, and I shivered to think of it. But again I recalled the teachings of my people, and determined to imitate their undaunted bravery and stoic resignation. However, I was far from having realized the long, tedious years of study and confinement before I could begin to achieve what I had planned.

"You must not fear to work with your hands," said my father, "but if you are able to think strongly and well, that will be a quiver full of arrows for you, my son. All of the white man's children must go to school, but those who study best and longest need not work with their hands after that, for they can work with their minds. You may plow the five acres next to the river, and see if you can make a straight furrow as well as a straight shot."

I set to work with the heavy breaking-plow and yoke of oxen, but I am sorry to admit that the work was poorly done. "It will be better for you to go away to a higher school," advised my father.

It appears remarkable to me now that my father, thorough Indian as he was, should have had such deep and sound conceptions of a true civilization. But there is the contrast—my father's mother! whose faith in her people's philosophy and training could not be superseded by any other allegiance.

To her such a life as we lead to-day would be no less than sacrilege. "It is not a true life," she often said. "It is a sham. I cannot bear to see my boy live a made-up life!"

Ah, grandmother! you had forgotten one of the first principles of your own teaching, namely: "When you see a new trail, or a footprint that you do not know, follow it to the point of knowing."

"All I want to say to you," the old grandmother seems to answer, "is this: Do not get lost on this new trail."

"I find," said my father to me, "that the white man has a well-grounded religion, and teaches his children the same virtues that our people taught to theirs. The Great Mystery has shown to the red and white man alike the good and evil, from which to choose. I think the way of the white man is better than ours, because he is able to preserve on paper the things he does not want to forget. He records everything—the sayings of his wise men, the laws enacted by his counselors."

I began to be really interested in this curious scheme of living that my father was gradually unfolding to me out of his limited experience.

"The way of knowledge," he continued, "is like our old way in hunting. You begin with a mere trail—a footprint. If you follow that faithfully, it may lead you to a clearer trail—a track—a road. Later on there will be many tracks, crossing and diverging one from the other. Then you must be careful, for success lies in the choice of the right road. You must be doubly careful, for traps will be laid for you, of which the most dangerous is the spirit-water, that causes a man to forget his self-respect," he added, unwittingly giving to his aged mother material for her argument against civilization.

The general effect upon me of these discussions, which were logical enough on the whole, although almost entirely from the outside, was that I became convinced that my father was right.

My grandmother had to yield at last, and it was settled that I was to go to school at Santee agency, Nebraska, where Dr. Alfred L. Riggs was then fairly started in the work of his great mission school, which has turned out some of the best educated Sioux Indians. It was at that time the Mecca of the Sioux country; even though Sitting Bull and Crazy Horse were still at large, harassing soldiers and emigrants alike, and General Custer had just been placed in military command of the Dakota Territory.

III. On the White Man's Trail

It was in the fall of 1874 that I started from Flandreau, then only an Indian settlement, with a good neighbor of ours on his way to Santee. There were only a dozen houses or so at Sioux Falls, and the whole country was practically uninhabited, when we embarked in a home-made prairie schooner, on that bright September morning.

I had still my Hudson Bay flintlock gun, which I had brought down with me from Canada the year before. I took that old companion, with my shot-pouch and a well-filled powder-horn. All I had besides was a blanket, and an extra shirt. I wore my hunting suit, which was a compromise between Indian attire and a frontiersman's outfit. I was about sixteen years old and small of my age.

"Remember, my boy, it is the same as if I sent you on your first war-path. I shall expect you to conquer," was my father's farewell. My good grandmother, who had brought me up as a motherless child, bestowed upon me her blessing. "Always remember," said she, "that the Great Mystery is good; evil can come only from ourselves!" Thus I parted with my first teacher—the woman who taught me to pray!

Our first night out was at Hole-in-the-Hill, one of the most picturesque spots in the valley. Here I brought in a doe, which I had come upon in the tall grass of the river bottom. Peter shot several ducks, and we had a good supper. It seemed to me more like one of our regular fall hunts than like going away to school.

After supper I said, "I am going to set some of your traps, uncle."

18

Santee Normal Training School, Santee, Nebraska, as it looks today.
No. 1 is the old Chapel; No. 2, the Dakota Home.

"And I will go with you," replied Peter, "But before we go, we must have our prayer," and he took out his Bible and hymn-book printed in the Indian tongue.

It was all odd enough to me, for although my father did the same, I had not yet become thoroughly used to such things. Nevertheless, it was the new era for the Indian; and while we were still seated on the ground around the central fire of the Sioux teepee, and had just finished our repast of wild game, Peter read from the good book, and performed the devotional exercises of his teepee home, with quite as much zeal as if he were within four walls and surrounded by civilized things. I was very much impressed when this primitive Christian prayed that I might succeed in my new undertaking.

The next morning was frosty, and after an early breakfast we hurried to our traps. I got two fine minks and a beaver for my trouble, while Peter came home smiling with two otters and three beaver. I saw that he had something on his mind, but, like a true Indian, I held my peace. At last he broke the news to me—he had changed his mind about going to Santee agency!

I did not blame him—it was hard to leave such a trapper's paradise as this, alive with signs of otter, mink, and beaver. I said nothing, but thought swiftly. The temptation was strong to remain and trap too. That would please my grandmother; and I will confess here that no lover is more keen to do the right thing for the loved one than I was at that time to please my old grandmother.

The thought of my father's wish kept me on my true course. Leaving my gun with Peter, I took my blanket on my back and started for the Missouri on foot.

"Tell my father," I said, "that I shall not return until I finish my war-path."

But the voice of the waterfall, near what is now the city of Sioux Falls, sounded like the spirits of woods and water crying for their lost playmate, and I thought for a moment of turning back to Canada, there to regain my freedom and wild life. Still, I had sent word to my father that this war-path should be completed, and I remembered how he had said that if I did not return, he would shed proud tears.

About this time I did some of the hardest thinking that I have ever done in my life. All day I traveled, and did not see any one until, late in the afternoon, descending into the valley of a stream, I came suddenly upon a solitary farm-house of sod, and was met by a white man—a man with much hair on his face.

I was hungry and thirsty as a moose in burned timber. I had some money that my father had given me—I hardly knew the different denominations; so I showed the man all of it, and told him by signs that he might take what he pleased if only he would let me have something to eat, and a little food to carry with me. As for lodging, I would not have slept in his house if he had promised me a war-bonnet!

While he was cordial—at any rate, after I exhibited my money—there was something about his manner that did not put me at my ease, and my wild instincts told me to keep an eye on him. But I was not alone in this policy, for his flock of four daughters and a son nearly put their necks out of joint in following my modest, shy movements.

When they invited me to sit down with them at the table, I felt uncomfortable, but hunger was stronger than my fears and modesty. The climax came when I took my seat on a rickety stool between the big, hairy man and one of his well-grown daughters. I felt not unlike a young blue heron just leaving the nest to partake of his first meal on an unsafe, swinging branch. I was entirely uncertain of my perch.

All at once, without warning, the man struck the table with the butt of his knife with such force that I jumped and was within an ace of giving a war-whoop. In spite of their taking a firm hold of the home-made table to keep it steady, the dishes were quivering, and the young ladies no longer able to maintain their composure. Severe glances from mother and father soon brought us calm, when it appeared that the blow on the table was merely a signal for quiet before saying grace. I pulled myself in, much as a turtle would do, and possibly it should be credited to the stoicism of my race that I scarcely ever ate a heartier meal.

After supper I got up and held out to the farmer nearly all the money I had. I did not care whether he took it all or not. I was grateful for the food, and money had no such hold on my mind as it has gained since. To my astonishment, he simply smiled, shook his head, and stroked his shaggy beard.

I was invited to join the family in the sod-house parlor, but owing to the severe nerve-shocks that I had experienced at the supper-table, I respectfully declined, and betook myself to the bank of the stream near by, where I sat down to meditate. Presently there pealed forth a peculiar, weird music, and the words of a strange song. It was music from a melodeon, but I did not then know what that was; and the tune was "Nearer, my God, to Thee." Strange as it sounded to me, I felt that there was something soothing and gentle about the music and the voices.

After a while curiosity led me back to the sod house, and I saw for the first time how the white woman pumps so much air into a box that when she presses on the top boards it howls convulsively. I forgot my bashfulness so far as to listen openly and enjoy the operation, wondering much how the white man puts a pair of lungs into a box, which is furnished with a whole set of black and white teeth, and when he sings to it, it appears to answer him.

Presently I walked over to a shed where the farmer seemed to be very busy with his son, earnestly hammering something with all their might in the midst of glowing fire and sparks. He had an old breaking-plow which he was putting into shape on his rude forge. With sleeves rolled up, face and hands blackened and streaming with sweat, I thought he looked not unlike a successful warrior just returned from the field of battle. His powerful muscles and the manly way in which he handled the iron impressed me tremendously. "I shall learn that profession if ever I reach the school and learn the white man's way," I thought.

I thanked the good man for his kind invitation to sleep within the sod walls with all his family, but signed to him that I preferred to sleep out-of-doors. I could see some distrust in his eyes, for his horses were in the open stable; and at that my temper rose, but I managed to control it. He had been kind to me, and no Indian will break the law of hospitality unless he has lost all the trails of his people. The man looked me over again carefully, and appeared satisfied; and I rolled myself up in my blanket among the willows, but every star that night seemed to be bent upon telling the story of the white man.

I slept little, and early the next morning I was awakened by the barking of the farmer's collie and the laughter of his daughters. I got up and came to the house. Breakfast was nearly ready, and every member of the family was on hand. After breakfast I once more offered my money, but was refused. I was glad. Then and there I loved civilization and renounced my wild life.

I took up my blanket and continued on my journey, which for three days was a lonely one. I had nothing with which to kill any game, so I stopped now and then at a sod house for food. When I reached the back hills of the Missouri, there lay before me a long slope leading to the river bottom, and upon the broad flat, as far as my eyes could reach, lay farm-houses and farms. Ah! I thought, this is the way of civilization, the basis upon which it rests! I desired to know that life.

Thirty miles from the school I met Dr. Riggs on the road, coming to the town of Yankton, and received some encouraging words from him, for he spoke the Sioux language very well. A little further on I met the Indian agent, Major Sears, a Quaker, and he, too, gave me a word of encouragement when he learned that I had walked a hundred and fifty miles to school. My older brother John, who was then assistant teacher and studying under Dr. Riggs, met me at the school and introduced me to my new life.

The bell of the old chapel at Santee summoned the pupils to class. Our principal read aloud from a large book and offered prayer. Although he conducted devotional exercises in the Sioux language, the subject matter was still strange, and the names he used were unintelligible to me. "Jesus" and "Jehovah" fell upon my ears as mere meaningless sounds.

I understood that he was praying to the "Great Mystery" that the work of the day might be blessed and their labor be fruitful. A cold sweat came out upon me as I heard him ask the "Great Mystery" to be with us in that day's work in that school building. I thought it was too much to ask of Him. I had been taught that the Supreme Being is only concerned with spirits, and that

Rev. Alfred L. Riggs, Superintendent Santee Training School.

when one wishes to commune with Him in nature he must be in a spiritual attitude, and must retire from human sound or influence, alone in the wilderness. Here for the first time I heard Him addressed openly in the presence of a house full of young men and young girls!

All the scholars were ordered to various rooms under different instructors, and I was left in the chapel with another long-haired young man. He was a Mandan from Fort Berthold—one of our ancient enemies. Not more than two years before that time my uncle had been on the war-path against this tribe and had brought home two Mandan scalps. He, too, was a new scholar, and looked as if he were about to come before the judge to receive his sentence. My heart at once went out to him, although the other pupils were all of my own tribe, the Sioux. I noticed that he had beautiful long hair arranged in two plaits, and in spite of his sad face he was noble-looking and appeared to great advantage, I thought, in contrast with the other pupils, whose hair was cut short and their garments not becoming to them at all. This boy, Alfred Mandan, became a very good friend of mine.

Dr. Riggs took me in hand and told me the rules of the school and what was expected of us. There was the chapel, which was used as a church every Sunday and as a schoolhouse on week days. There was the Dakota Home for the girls' dormitory—a small, square frame building—and for the boys a long log house some two hundred yards from the chapel under the large cottonwood-trees.

Dr. Riggs said that I need not study that first day, but could fill up the big bag he brought me with straw from the straw pile back of his barn. I carried it over to the log cabin, where the Doctor was before me and had provided a bunk or framework for my bed. I filled a smaller bag for a pillow, and, having received the sheets and blankets, I made my first white man's bed under his supervision. When it was done it looked clean and dignified enough for any one, I thought.

He said that I must make it every morning like that before going to school. "And for your wash, there is a tin basin or two on a bench just outside of the door, by the water-barrels." And so it was. We had three barrels of Missouri River water, which we ourselves filled up every week, for we boys had to furnish our own water and wood, and were detailed in pairs for this work.

Dr. Riggs supplied axes for the wood-choppers, and barrels and pails for the water-carriers, also a yoke of large and gentle white oxen and a lumber-wagon. It seems to me that I never was better acquainted with two animals than with these two! I have done some of my solemnest thinking behind them. The Missouri River was about two miles from our log house, with a wide stretch of bottom land intervening, partly cottonwood timber and partly open meadow with tall grass. I could take a nap, or dance a war-dance, if I cared to do so, while they were carrying me to wood or to water.

Dr. Riggs gave me a little English primer to study, also one or two books in the Dakota language, which I had learned to read in the day-school. There was a translation of the Psalms, and of the Pilgrim's Progress. I must confess that at that time I would have preferred one of grandmother's evening stories, or my uncle's account of his day's experiences in the chase. I thought it was the dullest hunting I had ever known!

Toward evening a company of three young men arrived from up the river—to all appearance full-fledged warriors. Ah, it was good to see the handsome white, blue, and red blankets worn by these stately Sioux youths! I had not worn one since my return from Canada. My brother got me a suit of clothes, and had some one cut my hair, which was already over my ears, as it had not been touched since the year before. I felt like a wild goose with its wings clipped.

Next morning the day pupils emerged in every direction from the woods and deep ravines where the Indians had made their temporary homes, while we, the log-cabin boarders, came out in Indian file. The chapel bell was tolling as we reached the yard, when my attention was attracted to a pretty lass standing with her parents and Dr. Riggs near the Dakota Home. Then they separated and the father and mother came toward us, leaving the Doctor and the pretty Dakota maiden standing still. All at once the girl began to run toward her parents, screaming pitifully.

"Oh, I cannot, I cannot stay in the white man's house! I'll die, I'll die! Mamma! Mamma!"

The parents stopped and reasoned with the girl, but it was of no use. Then I saw them leading her back to the Dakota Home, in spite of her pleading and begging. The scene made my blood boil, and I suppressed with difficulty a strong desire to go to her aid.

How well I remember the first time we were called upon to recite! In the same primer class were Eagle-Crane, Kite, and their compatriot from up the river. For a whole week we youthful warriors were held up and harassed with words of three letters. Like raspberry bushes in the path, they tore, bled, and sweated us—those little words rat, cat, and so forth—until not a semblance of our native dignity and self-respect was left. And we were of just the age when the Indian youth is most on his dignity! Imagine the same fellows turned loose against Custer or Harney with anything like equal numbers and weapons, and those tried generals would feel like boys! We had been bred and trained to those things; but when we found ourselves within four walls and set to pick out words of three letters we were like novices upon snow-shoes—often flat on the ground.

I hardly think I was ever tired in my life until those first days of boarding-school. All day things seemed to come and pass with a wearisome regularity, like walking railway ties—the step was too short for me. At times I felt something of the fascination of the new life, and again there would arise in me a dogged resistance, and a voice seemed to be saying, "It is cowardly to depart from the old things!"

Aside from repeating and spelling words, we had to count and add imaginary accounts. We never had had any money to count, nor potatoes, nor turnips, nor bricks. Why, we valued nothing except honor; that cannot be purchased! It seemed now that everything must be measured in time or money or distance. And when the teacher placed before us a painted globe, and said that our world was like that—that upon such a thing our forefathers had roamed and hunted for untold ages, as it whirled and danced around the sun in space—I felt that my foothold was deserting me. All my savage training and philosophy was in the air, if these things were true.

Later on, when Dr. Riggs explained to us the industries of the white man, his thrift and forethought, we could see the reasonableness of it all. Economy is the able assistant of labor, and the two together produce great results. The systems and methods of business were of great interest to us, and especially the adoption of a medium of exchange.

The Doctor's own personality impressed us deeply, and his words of counsel and daily prayers, strange to us at first, in time found root in our minds. Next to my own father, this man did more than perhaps any other to make it possible for me to grasp the principles of true civilization. He also strengthened and developed in me that native strong ambition to win out, by sticking to whatever I might undertake. Associated with him was another man who influenced me powerfully toward Christian living. This was the Rev. Dr. John P. Williamson, the pioneer Presbyterian missionary. The world seemed gradually to unfold before me, and the desire to know all that the white man knows was the tremendous and prevailing thought in me, and was constantly growing upon me more and more.

My father wrote to me in the Dakota language for my encouragement. Dr. Riggs had told him that I was not afraid of books or of work, but rather determined to profit by them. "My son," he wrote, "I believe that an Indian can learn all that is in the books of the white man, so that he may be equal to them in the ways of the mind!"

I studied harder than most of the boys. Missionaries were poor, and the Government policy of education for the Indian had not then been developed. The white man in general had no use for the Indian. Sitting Bull and the Northern Cheyennes were still fighting in Wyoming and Montana, so that the outlook was not bright for me to pursue my studies among the whites, yet it was now my secret dream and ambition.

It was at Santee that I sawed my first cord of wood. Before long I had a little money of my own, for I sawed most of Dr. Riggs's own wood and some at the Dakota Home, besides other work for which I was paid. Although I could not understand or speak much English, at the end of my second year I could translate every word of my English studies into the native tongue, besides having read all that was then published in the Sioux. I had caught up with boys who had two or three years the start of me, and was now studying elementary algebra and geometry.

One day Dr. Riggs came to me and said that he had a way by which he could send me to Beloit, Wisconsin, to enter the preparatory department of Beloit College. This was a great opportunity, and I grasped it eagerly, though I had not yet lost my old timidity about venturing alone among the white people.

On the eve of departure, I received word from Flandreau that my father was dead, after only two days' illness. He was still in the prime of life and a tireless worker. This was a severe shock to me, but I felt even more strongly that I must carry out his wishes. It was clear that he who had sought me out among the wild tribes at the risk of his life, and set my feet in the new trail, should be obeyed to the end. I did not go back to my home, but in September, 1876, I started from Santee to Beloit to begin my serious studies.

IV. College Life in the West

The journey to Beloit College was an education in itself. At Yankton City I boarded the train for the first time in my life, but not before having made a careful inspection of the locomotive—that fiery monster which had so startled me on my way home from Canada. Every hour brought new discoveries and new thoughts—visions that came and passed like the telegraph poles as we sped by. More and more we seemed to me to be moving upon regions too small for the inhabitants. Towns and villages grew ever larger and nearer together, until at last we reached a city of some little size where it was necessary for me to change cars, a matter that had been arranged by Dr. Riggs with the conductor. The streets looked crowded and everybody seemed to be in the greatest possible hurry. I was struck with the splendor of the shops and the brilliant show windows. Some one took me to an eating house and left me alone with the pretty waitress, whose bright eyes and fluent speech alarmed me. I thought it best to agree with everything she said, so I assented with a nod of the head, and I fancy she brought me everything that was on the bill of fare!

When I reached Beloit on the second day of my pilgrimage, I found it beautifully located on the high, wooded banks of Black Hawk's picturesque Rock River. The college grounds covered the site of an ancient village of mound-builders, which showed to great advantage on the neat campus, where the green grass was evenly cut with lawn-mowers. I was taken to President Chapin's house, and after a kindly greeting, shown to my room in South College, where I immediately opened all the windows.

A young man emerged from our building and I could distinctly hear him shouting to another across the Common:

"Hurry up, Turkey, or you'll not have the chance to face old Petty again! We have Sitting Bull's nephew right here, and it's more than likely he'll have your scalp-lock before morning!"

"Turkey," as I soon learned, was the son of a missionary to that country, and both of these boys became good friends of mine afterward.

It must be remembered that this was September, 1876, less than three months after Custer's gallant command was annihilated by the hostile Sioux. I was especially troubled when I learned that my two uncles whom we left in Canada had taken part in this famous fight. People were bitter against the Sioux in those days, and I think it was a local paper that printed the story that I was a nephew of Sitting Bull, who had sent me there to study the white man's arts so that he might be better able to cope with him. When I went into the town, I was followed on the streets by gangs of little white savages, giving imitation war whoops.

My first recitation at Beloit was an event in my life. I was brought before a remarkable looking man whose name was Professor Pettibone. He had a long, grave face, with long whiskers and scarcely any hair on his head, and was to me the very embodiment of wisdom. I was already well drilled in the elementary studies, except that I was very diffident about speaking the English language, and found it hard to recite or to demonstrate mathematical problems. However, I made every effort and soon learned to speak quite fluently, although not correctly; but that fact did not discourage me.

I was now a stranger in a strange country, and deep in a strange life from which I could not retreat. I was like a deaf man with eyes continually on the alert for the expression of faces, and to find them in general friendly toward me was somewhat reassuring. In spite of some nerve-trying moments, I soon recovered my balance and set to work. I absorbed knowledge through every pore. The more I got, the larger my capacity grew, and my appetite increased in proportion. I discovered that my anticipations of this new life were nearly all wrong, and was suddenly confronted with problems entirely foreign to my experience. If I had been told to swim across a lake, or run with a message through an unknown country, I should have had some conception of the task; but the idea of each word as having an office and a place and a specific name, and standing in relation to other words like the bricks in a wall, was almost beyond my grasp. As for history and geography, to me they were legends and traditions, and I soon learned to appreciate the pure logic of mathematics. A recent letter from a Beloit schoolmate says, "You were the only boy who could beat me in algebra!"

At Beloit I spent three years of student life. While in some kinds of knowledge I was the infant of the college, in athletics I did my full share. To keep myself at my best physically, I spent no less than three hours daily in physical exercise, and this habit was kept up throughout my college days.

I found among the students many who were self-supporting, either the sons of poor parents, or self-reliant youth who preferred to earn money for at least a part of their expenses. I soon discovered that these young men were usually among the best students. Since I had no means of my own, and the United States Government had not then formulated the policy of Indian education, I was ready for any kind of work, and on Saturdays I usually sawed wood and did other chores for the professors.

During the first summer vacation I determined to hire out to a farmer. Armed with a letter of introduction from President Chapin, I set out in a southerly direction. As I walked, I recalled the troubles of that great chief of the Sac and Fox tribe, Black Hawk, who had some dispute with President Lincoln about that very region.

At the first farm I came to, I approached the front door with some misgivings. A young lady asked me to wait, and I fancied I read in her clear blue eyes the thoughts that passed through her mind. In ten minutes or so, the farmer came in from the field and entered his home by another door, apparently taking some precautions against a surprise before coming to me where I waited, hungry and tired, on the doorstep.

"Well, young man, what do you want?" quoth he.

I said, "I am a student at Beloit College, but the college is closed for the summer and I am looking for work."

"Oho! you can not work the New Ulm game on me. I don't think you can reproduce the Fort Dearborn massacre on this farm. By the way, what tribe do you belong to?"

"I am Sioux," I replied.

"That settles it. Get off from my farm just as quick as you can! I had a cousin killed by your people only last summer."

I kept on my way until I found another farmer to whom I made haste to present my letter. For him I worked all summer, and as treaties were kept on both sides, there was no occasion for any trouble.

It was here and now that my eyes were opened intelligently to the greatness of Christian civilization, the ideal civilization, as it unfolded itself before my eyes. I saw it as the development of every natural resource; the broad brotherhood of mankind; the blending of all languages and the gathering of all races under one religious faith. There must be no more warfare within our borders; we must quit the forest trail for the breaking-plow, since pastoral life was the next thing for the Indian. I renounced finally my bow and arrows for the spade and the pen; I took off my soft moccasins and put on the heavy and clumsy but durable shoes. Every day of my life I put into use every English word that I knew, and for the first time permitted myself to think and act as a white man.

At the end of three years, other Sioux Indians had been sent to Beloit, and I felt that I might progress faster where I was not surrounded by my tribesmen. Dr. Riggs arranged to transfer me to the preparatory department of Knox College, at Galesburg, Ill., of which he was himself a graduate. Here, again, I was thrown into close contact with the rugged, ambitious sons of western farmers. Among my stanch friends at Knox were S. S. McClure, John S. Phillips of the *American Magazine*, Edgar A. Bancroft of Chicago, now attorney for the International Harvester Company, Judge Merritt Pinckney of Chicago, Representative Rainey, and other men who have become well known and whose friendship is still retained.

As Knox is a co-educational institution, it was here that I

mingled for the first time with the pale-face maidens, and as
soon as I could shake off my Indian shyness, I found them very
winning and companionable. It was through social intercourse
with the American college girl that I gained my first conception
of the home life and domestic ideals of the white man. I had
thoroughly learned the Indian club and dumb bell exercises at
Beloit, and here at Knox I was enabled by teaching them to a
class of young ladies to meet a part of my expenses.

Soon I began to lay definite plans for the future. Happily, I
had missed the demoralizing influences of reservation life, and
had been mainly thrown with the best class of Christian white
people. With all the strength of a clean young manhood, I set
my heart upon the completion of a liberal education.

The next question to decide was what should be my special
work in life. It appeared that in civilization one must have a definite occupation—a profession. I wished to share with my people whatever I might attain, and I looked about me for a distinct
field of usefulness apart from the ministry, which was the first to
be adopted by the educated Sioux.

Gradually my choice narrowed down to law and medicine, for
both of which I had a strong taste; but the latter seemed to me
to offer a better opportunity of service to my race; therefore I
determined upon the study of medicine long before I entered
upon college studies. "Hitch your wagon to a star," says the
American philosopher, and this was my star!

V. College Life in the East

O ne summer vacation, at my home in Dakota, Dr. Riggs told
me the story of Dartmouth College in New Hampshire,
and how it was originally founded as a school for Indian youth.
The news was timely and good news; and yet I hesitated. I
dreaded to cut myself off from my people, and in my heart I
knew that if I went, I should not return until I had accomplished
my purpose. It was a critical moment in my life, but the decision
could be only one way. I taught the little day-school where my
first lessons had been learned, throughout the fall term, and in
January, 1882, I set out for the far East, at a period when the
Government was still at considerable trouble to subdue and set-
tle some of my race upon reservations.

Though a man in years, I had very little practical knowledge
of the world, and in my inexperience I was still susceptible to
the adventurous and curious side of things rather than to their
profounder meanings. Therefore, while somewhat prepared, I
was not yet conscious of the seriousness and terrific power of
modern civilization.

It was a crisp winter morning when the train pulled into
Chicago. I had in mind the Fort Dearborn incident, and it
seemed to me that we were being drawn into the deep gulches
of the Bad Lands as we entered the city. I realized vividly at that
moment that the day of the Indian had passed forever.

I was met at the station by friends, who took me to walk upon
some of the main streets. I saw a perfect stream of humanity
rushing madly along, and noticed with some surprise that the

faces of the people were not happy at all. They wore an intensely serious look that to me was appalling.

I was cautioned against trusting strangers, and told that I must look out for pickpockets. Evidently there were some disadvantages connected with this mighty civilization, for we Indians seldom found it necessary to guard our possessions. It seemed to me that the most dignified men on the streets were the policemen, in their long blue coats with brass buttons. They were such a remarkable set of men physically that this of itself was enough to catch my eye.

Soon I was again upon the eastern bound express, and we had not gone far when a middle-aged man who had thoroughly investigated my appearance both through and over his glasses, came to my seat and without apology or introduction began to bombard me with countless questions.

"You are an Indian?" he began.

"Yes," I murmured.

"What is your tribe?"

"Sioux."

"How came you so far away from the tribe? Are you a member of Sitting Bull's band? Are you related to him?" he continued. I was greatly relieved when he released me from his intrusive scrutiny. Among our people, the children and old women sometimes betray curiosity as regards a stranger, but no grown man would be guilty of such bad manners as I have often met with when traveling.

After we left Albany, I found myself in a country the like of which, I thought, I would have given much to hunt over before it was stripped of its primeval forests, and while deer and bears roamed over it undisturbed. I looked with delight upon mountains and valleys, and even the little hamlets perched upon the shelves of the high hills. The sight of these rocky farms and little villages reminded me of the presence of an earnest and persistent people. Even the deserted farmhouse, the ruined mill, had an air of saying, "I have done my part in the progress of civilization. Now I can rest." And all the mountains seemed to say, Amen.

What is the great difference between these people and my

own? I asked myself. Is it not that the one keeps the old things and continually adds to them new improvements, while the other is too well contented with the old, and will not change his ways nor seek to improve them?

When I reached Boston, I was struck with the old, mossy, granite edifices, and the narrow, crooked streets. Here, too, the people hurried along as if the gray wolf were on their trail. Their ways impressed me as cold, but I forgot that when I had learned to know some of them better.

I went on to Dartmouth College, away up among the granite hills. The country around it is rugged and wild; and thinking of the time when red men lived here in plenty and freedom, it seemed as if I had been destined to come view their graves and bones. No, I said to myself, I have come to continue that which in their last struggle they proposed to take up, in order to save themselves from extinction; but alas! it was too late. Had our New England tribes but followed the example of that great Indian, Samson Occum, and kept up with the development of Dartmouth College, they would have brought forth leaders and men of culture. This was my ambition—that the Sioux should accept civilization before it was too late! I wished that our young men might at once take up the white man's way, and prepare themselves to hold office and wield influence in their native states. Although this hope has not been fully realized, I have the satisfaction of knowing that not a few Indians now hold positions of trust and exercise some political power.

At Dartmouth College I found the buildings much older and more imposing than any I had seen before. There was a true scholastic air about them; in fact, the whole village impressed me as touched with the spirit of learning and refinement. My understanding of English was now so much enlarged as to enable me to grasp current events, as well as the principles of civilization, in a more intelligent manner.

At Kimball Union Academy, the little ancient institution at which I completed my preparation for college by direction of President Bartlett of Dartmouth, I absorbed much knowledge of the New Englander and his peculiarities. I found Yankees of the uneducated class very Indian-like in their views and habits;

a people of strong character, plain-spoken, and opinionated. However, I observed that the students of the academy and their parents were very frugal and saving. Nothing could have been more instructive to me, as we Indians are inclined to be improvident. I had been accustomed to broad, fertile prairies, and liberal ways. Here they seemed to count their barrels of potatoes and apples before they were grown. Every little brooklet was forced to do a river's work in their mills and factories.

I was graduated here and went to old Dartmouth in the fall of 1883 to enter the Freshman class. Although I had associated with college students for several years, yet I must confess that western college life is quiet compared with that of the tumultuous East. It was here that I had most of my savage gentleness and native refinement knocked out of me. I do not complain, for I know that I gained more than their equivalent.

On the evening of our first class meeting, lo! I was appointed football captain for my class. My supporters orated quite effectively on my qualifications as a frontier warrior, and some went so far as to predict that I would, when warmed up, scare all the Sophs off the premises! These representations seemed to be confirmed when, that same evening after supper, the two classes met in a first "rush," and as I was not acquainted with the men, I held up the professor of philosophy, mistaking him for one of the sophomores. Reporters for the Boston dailies made the most of their opportunity to enlarge upon this incident.

I was a sort of prodigal son of old Dartmouth, and nothing could have exceeded the heartiness of my welcome. The New England Indians, for whom it was founded, had departed well-nigh a century earlier, and now a warlike Sioux, like a wild fox, had found his way into this splendid seat of learning! Though poor, I was really better off than many of the students, since the old college took care of me under its ancient charter. I was treated with the greatest kindness by the president and faculty, and often encouraged to ask questions and express my own ideas. My uncle's observations in natural history, for which he had a positive genius, the Indian standpoint in sociology and political economy, these were the subject of some protracted discussions in the class room. This became so well understood,

PART OF CLASS OF '87, DARTMOUTH COLLEGE, AFTER A "RUSH." EASTMAN IN CENTRE, FRONT.

that some of my classmates who had failed to prepare their recitations would induce me to take up the time by advancing a native theory or first hand observation.

For the first time, I became really interested in literature and history. Here it was that civilization began to loom up before me colossal in its greatness, when the fact dawned upon me that nations and tongues, as well as individuals, have lived and died. There were two men of the past who were much in my thoughts: my countryman Occum, who matriculated there a century before me, and the great Daniel Webster (said to have a strain of Indian blood), who came to Dartmouth as impecunious as I was. It was under the Old Pine Tree that the Indians were supposed to have met for the last time to smoke the pipe of peace, and under its shadow every graduating class of my day smoked a parting pipe.

I was anxious to help myself as much as possible and gain practical experience at the same time, by working during the long summer vacations. One summer I worked in a hotel, at another time I canvassed for a book, I think it was the "Knights of Labor," published in Boston. Such success as I attained was due less to any business sagacity than to a certain curiosity I seemed to excite, and which often resulted in the purchase of the book, whether the subscriber really cared for it or not. Another summer, an old school friend, an Armenian, conceived the scheme of dressing me in native costume and sending me out to sell his goods. When I wore a jacket and fez, and was well scented with attar of rose, no dog would permit me on his master's premises if he could help it; nevertheless I did very well. For business purposes I was a Turk, but I never answered any direct questions on the subject of my nativity.

Throughout my student days in the West, I had learned to reverence New England, and especially its metropolis, as the home of culture and art, of morality and Christianity. At that period that sort of thing got a lodging place in my savage mind more readily than the idea of wealth or material power. Somehow I had supposed that Boston must be the home of the nation's elect and not far from the millenium. I was very happy when, after my graduation with the class of 1887, it was made possible for me to study medicine at Boston University. The friends who generously assisted me to realize my great ambition were of the type I had dreamed of, and my home influences in their family all that I could have wished for. A high ideal of duty was placed before me, and I was doubly armed in my original purpose to make my education of service to my race. I continued to study the Christ philosophy and loved it for its essential truths, though doctrines and dogmas often puzzled and repelled me. I attended the Shawmut Congregational church, of which the Rev. William Eliot Griffis was then pastor, and I am happy to say he became my life-long friend.

Mr. and Mrs. Frank Wood, who were a father and mother to me at this period of my life, were very considerate of my health and gave me opportunity to enter into many outdoor sports, such as tennis and canoeing, beside regular gymnasium work. The unique features of old Boston, the park system with the public flower gardens and the Arboretum, the reservoirs, and above all, the harbor with its vast assemblage of vessels, each of these was a school in itself. I did much general reading, and did not neglect my social opportunities. At Dartmouth I had met the English man of letters, Matthew Arnold, and he was kind enough to talk with me for some time. I have also talked with Emerson, Longfellow, Francis Parkman, and many other men of note. Mr. and Mrs. Wood were trustees of Wellesley College and I was so fortunate as to be an occasional visitor there, and to make the acquaintance of Miss Freeman, its first president. I believe the first lecture I ever delivered in public was before the Wellesley girls. I little dreamed that a daughter of mine would ever be among them! At another time I was asked by Mrs. Hemenway to give one of a course of eight historical lectures to the high school boys and girls. My subject was the French and Indian wars, especially the conspiracy of Pontiac. I had studied this period minutely and spoke for an hour and a quarter without any manuscript.

At the seaside hotels, I met society people of an entirely different sort to those I had hitherto taken as American types. I was, I admit, particularly struck with the audacity and forwardness of the women. Among our people the man always leads. I

MRS. FRANK WOOD, OF BOSTON. EASTMAN'S "WHITE MOTHER."

was astonished to learn that some women whom I had observed to accept the most marked attentions from the men were married ladies. Perhaps my earlier training had been too Puritanical, or my æsthetic sense was not then fully developed, for I was surprised when I entered the ballroom to see the pretty women clad so scantily.

One summer at Nantasket beach, I recall that I had somehow been noted by an enterprising representative of a Boston daily, who printed a column or so on my doings, which were innocent enough. He good-naturedly remarked that "the hero of the Boston society girls just now is a Sioux brave," etc. and described all the little gifts of sofa cushions, pictures, and so on, that I had ever received from my girl friends, as well as the medals won in college. I never knew who had let him into my room!

During the three years that I studied in Boston, I went every summer to Mr. Moody's famous summer school at Northfield, and was much interested in his strong personality. One morning as we walked together, we came to a stone at the roadside. "Eastman," said he, "this stone is a reminder of the cruelty of your countrymen two centuries ago. Here they murdered an innocent Christian."

"Mr. Moody," I replied, "it might have been better if they had killed them all. Then you would not have had to work so hard to save the souls of their descendants."

At the date of my graduation, in 1890, the Government had fully committed itself to the new and permanent plan of educating the young Indians preparatory to admitting them to citizenship. Various philanthropic societies had been formed expressly to help toward this end. These facts gave weight and momentum to my desire to use all that I had learned for their benefit. I soon received my appointment to the position of Government physician at Pine Ridge agency in South Dakota, to report October first. Meantime I stayed in Boston and kept books for Mr. Wood while his bookkeeper took a vacation, and later secured an extension of time in order to attend the Lake Mohonk Indian conference. Here I met Mr. Herbert Welsh and Professor Painter of the Indian Rights association, Bishop Hare,

Bishop Whipple, and many others, and listened with great interest to their discussions. I became convinced that the Indians had some real friends and this gave me much encouragement.

VI. A Doctor among the Indians

The Pine Ridge Indian agency was a bleak and desolate looking place in those days, more especially in a November dust
storm such as that in which I arrived from Boston to take charge
of the medical work of the reservation. In 1890 a "white doctor"
who was also an Indian was something of a novelty, and I was
afterward informed that there were many and diverse specula-
tions abroad as to my success or failure in this new rôle, but at
the time I was unconscious of an audience. I was thirty-two
years of age, but appeared much younger, athletic and vigorous,
and alive with energy and enthusiasm.

After reporting to the Indian agent, I was shown to my quarters, which consisted of a bedroom, sitting room, office, and dispensary, all in one continuous barrack with the police quarters
and the agent's offices. This barrack was a flimsy one-story affair
built of warped cottonwood lumber, and the rude prairie winds
whistled musically through the cracks. There was no carpet, no
furniture save a plain desk and a couple of hard wooden chairs,
and everything was coated with a quarter of an inch or so of fine
Dakota dust. This did not disconcert me, however, as I myself
was originally Dakota dust! An old-fashioned box stove was the
only cheerful thing on the premises, and the first duty I performed was to myself. I built a roaring fire in the stove, and sat
down for a few minutes to take a sort of inventory of the situation and my professional prospects.

I had not yet thought seriously of making a life contract with
any young woman, and accordingly my place was at the agency
mess where the unmarried employees took their meals. I recall

45

EASTMAN AT KNOX COLLEGE, 1880.

EASTMAN IN 1890, WHEN HE TOOK HIS
MEDICAL DEGREE AT BOSTON UNIVERSITY.

that the cook at that time was a German, and the insistent sauer-kraut and other German dishes were new to me and not especially appetizing.

After supper, as I sat alone in my dismal quarters fighting the first pangs of homesickness, an Indian softly opened the door and stepped in without knocking, in characteristic Indian fashion. My first caller was old Blue Horse, chief emeritus of the Loafer band, of which American Horse was the active chief. After greeting me in Sioux, he promptly produced his credentials, which consisted of well-worn papers that had been given him by various high military officers, from General Harney to General Crook, and were dated 1854 to 1877. Blue Horse had been, as he claimed, a friend to the white man, for he was one of the first Sioux army scouts, and also one of the first to cross the ocean with Buffalo Bill. The old man wanted nothing so much as an audience, and the tale of his exploits served to pass the evening. Some one had brought in a cot and an armful of blankets, and I was soon asleep.

Next morning I hunted up an Indian woman to assist in a general cleaning and overhauling of the premises. My first official act was to close up the "hole in the wall," like a ticket seller's window, through which my predecessors had been wont to deal out pills and potions to a crowd of patients standing in line, and put a sign outside the door telling them to come in.

It so happened that this was the day of the "Big Issue," on which thousands of Indians scattered over a reservation a hundred miles long by fifty wide, came to the agency for a weekly or fortnightly supply of rations, and it was a veritable "Wild West" array that greeted my astonished eyes. The streets and stores were alive with a motley crowd in picturesque garb, for all wore their best on these occasions. Every road leading to the agency was filled with white-topped lumber wagons, with here and there a more primitive travois, and young men and women on ponies' backs were gaily curvetting over the hills. The Sioux belle of that period was arrayed in grass-green or bright purple calico, loaded down with beads and bangles, and sat astride a spotted pony, holding over her glossy uncovered braids and vermilion-tinted cheeks a gaily colored silk parasol.

Toward noon, the whole population moved out two or three miles to a large corral in the midst of a broad prairie, where a herd of beef cattle was held in readiness by the agency cowboys. An Indian with stentorian voice, mounted on a post, announced the names of the group whose steer was to be turned loose. Next moment the flying animal was pursued by two or three swift riders with rifles across their saddles. As the cattle were turned out in quick succession, we soon had a good imitation of the old time buffalo hunt. The galloping, long-horned steers were chased madly in every direction, amid yells and whoops, the firing of guns and clouds of yellow dust, with here and there a puff of smoke and a dull report as one stumbled and fell.

The excitement was soon over, and men of each group were busy skinning the animals, dressing the meat and dividing it among the families interested. Meanwhile the older women, sack in hand, approached the commissary, where they received their regular dole of flour, bacon, coffee, and sugar. Fires were soon blazing merrily in the various temporary camps scattered over the prairie and in the creek bottoms, and after dinner, horse races and dancing were features of the day. Many white sight-seers from adjoining towns were usually on hand. Before night, most of the people had set off in a cloud of dust for their distant homes.

It is no wonder that I was kept on my feet giving out medicine throughout that day, as if from a lemonade stand at a fair. It was evident that many were merely seeking an excuse to have a look at the "Indian white doctor." Most of them diagnosed their own cases and called for some particular drug or ointment; a mixture of cod liver oil and alcohol was a favorite. It surprised them that I insisted upon examining each patient and questioning him in plain Sioux—no interpreter needed! I made a record of the interesting cases and took note of the place where they were encamped, planning to visit as many as possible in their teepees before they took again to the road.

The children of the large Government boarding school were allowed to visit their parents on issue day, and when the parting moment came, there were some pathetic scenes. It was one of my routine duties to give written excuses from school when

CHAPEL OF THE HOLY CROSS, PINE RIDGE AGENCY, USED AS HOSPITAL
FOR WOUNDED INDIANS DURING THE "GHOST DANCE WAR."

PINE RIDGE AGENCY, 1890.

necessary on the ground of illness, and these excuses were in much demand from lonely mothers and homesick little ones. As a last resort, the mother herself would sometimes plead illness and the need of her boy or girl for a few days at home. I was of course wholly in sympathy with the policy of education for the Indian children, yet by no means hardened to the exhibition of natural feeling. I would argue the matter with the parents as tactfully as I could; but if nothing else could win the coveted paper, the grandmother was apt to be pressed into the service, and her verbal ammunition seemed inexhaustible.

Captain Sword, the dignified and intelligent head of the Indian police force, was very friendly, and soon found time to give me a great deal of information about the place and the people. He said finally:

"Kola (my friend), the people are very glad that you have come. You have begun well; we Indians are all your friends. But I fear that we are going to have trouble. I must tell you that a new religion has been proclaimed by some Indians in the Rocky Mountain region, and some time ago, Sitting Bull sent several of his men to investigate. We hear that they have come back, saying that they saw the prophet, or Messiah, who told them that he is God's Son whom He has sent into the world a second time. He told them that He had waited nearly two thousand years for the white men to carry out His teachings, but instead they had destroyed helpless small nations to satisfy their own selfish greed. Therefore He had come again, this time as a Savior to the red people. If they would follow His instructions exactly, in a little while He would cause the earth to shake and destroy all the cities of the white man, when famine and pestilence would come to finish the work. The Indians must live entirely by themselves in their teepees so that the earthquake would not harm them. They must fast and pray and keep up a holy or spirit dance that He taught them. He also ordered them to give up the white man's clothing and make shirts and dresses in the old style.

"My friend," Sword went on, "our reservation has been free from this new teaching until the last few weeks. Quite lately this ghost dance was introduced by Slow Bull and Kicking Bear from

Rosebud"—a neighboring agency. "It has been rapidly gaining converts in many of the camps. This is what the council to-day was about. The agent says that the Great Father at Washington wishes it stopped. I fear the people will not stop. I fear trouble, kola."

I listened in silence, for I was taken entirely by surprise. Shortly afterward, the agent himself, a new man and a political appointee, approached me on the same matter. "I tell you, doctor," he began, after an exchange of greetings, "I am mighty glad you came here at just this time. We have a most difficult situation to handle, but those men down in Washington don't seem to realize the facts. If I had my way, I would have had troops here before this," he declared with emphasis. "This Ghost dance craze is the worst thing that has ever taken hold of the Indian race. It is going like wild fire among the tribes, and right here and now the people are beginning to defy my authority, and my Indian police seem to be powerless. I expect every employee on the agency to do his or her best to avert an outbreak." I assured him that he might count on me. "I shall talk to you more fully on the subject as soon as you are settled," he concluded.

I began to think the situation must be serious, and decided to consult some of the educated and Christian Indians. At this juncture a policeman appeared with a note, and handed me my orders, as I supposed. But when I opened it, I read a gracefully worded welcome and invitation to a tea party at the rectory, "to celebrate," the writer said, "my birthday, and your coming to Pine Ridge." I was caught up by the wind of destiny, but at the moment my only thought was of pleasure in the prospect of soon meeting the Reverend Charles Smith Cook, the Episcopal missionary. He was a Yankton Sioux, a graduate of Trinity College and Seabury Divinity School, and I felt sure that I should find in him a congenial friend.

I looked forward to the evening with a peculiar interest. Mr. Cook was delightful, and so was his gracious young wife, who had been a New York girl. She had a sweet voice and was a trained musician. They had a little boy three or four years old. Then I met several young ladies, teachers in the boarding school, and a young man or two, and finally Miss Elaine

Goodale, who was not entirely a stranger, as I had read her "Apple Blossoms" in Boston, and some of her later articles on Indian education in the *Independent* and elsewhere. Miss Goodale was supervisor of Indian schools in the Dakotas and Nebraska, and she was then at Pine Ridge on a tour of inspection. She was young for such a responsible position, but appeared equal to it in mentality and experience. I thought her very dignified and reserved, but this first evening's acquaintance showed me that she was thoroughly in earnest and absolutely sincere in her work for the Indians. I might as well admit that her personality impressed me deeply. I had laid my plans carefully, and purposed to serve my race for a few years in my profession, after which I would go to some city to practice, and I had decided that it would be wise not to think of marriage for the present. I had not given due weight to the possibility of love.

Events now crowded fast upon one another. It would seem enough that I had at last realized the dream of my life—to be of some service to my people—an ambition implanted by my earlier Indian teachers and fostered by my missionary training. I was really happy in devoting myself mind and body to my hundreds of patients who left me but few leisure moments. I soon found it absolutely necessary to have some help in the dispensary, and I enlisted the aid of George Graham, a Scotch half-breed, and a simple, friendly fellow. I soon taught him to put up the common salves and ointments, the cough syrups and other mixtures which were in most frequent demand. Together we scoured the shelves from top to bottom and prepared as best we could for the issue day crowds.

After the second "Big Issue," I had another call from Captain Sword. He began, I believe, by complimenting me upon a very busy day. "Your reputation," he declared, "has already travelled the length and breadth of the reservation. You treat everybody alike, and your directions are understood by the people. No Government doctor has ever gone freely among them before. It is a new order of things. But I fear you have come at a bad time," he added seriously. "The Ghost dancers have not heeded the agent's advice and warning. They pay no attention to us policemen. The craze is spreading like a prairie fire, and the chiefs who are encouraging it do not even come to the agency. They send after their rations and remain at home. It looks bad."

"Do they really mean mischief?" I asked incredulously, for Mr. Cook and I had discussed the matter and agreed in thinking that if the attempt was not made to stop it by force, the craze would die out of itself before long.

"They say not, and that all they ask is to be let alone. They say the white man is not disturbed when he goes to church," Sword replied. "I must tell you, however, that the agent has just ordered the police to call in all Government employees with their families to the agency. This means that something is going to happen. I have heard that he will send for soldiers to come here to stop the Ghost dance. If so, there will be trouble."

As I was still too new to the situation to grasp it fully, I concluded that in any case the only thing for me to do was to apply myself diligently to my special work, and await the issue. I had arranged to give a course of simple talks on physiology and hygiene at the Government boarding school, and on the evening of my first talk, I came back to my quarters rather late, for I had been invited to join the teachers afterward in their reading circle, and had then seen Miss Goodale safe to the rectory.

I had given up two of my rooms to Colonel Lee, the census taker, and his wife, who could find no other shelter in the crowded state of the agency, and found them awaiting me.

"Well, doc," said the jolly Colonel, "I suppose you have fixed your eye on the prettiest of the school teachers by this time!"

"I should be a callous man if I hadn't," I laughed.

"That's the right spirit. And now, here's a big bundle the stage left for you. Open it up, doc; it may be some pies or Boston baked beans from your folks!"

The parcel contained a riding suit of corduroy lined with leather, and reversible, also a pair of laced riding-boots reaching to the thigh, a present from an old friend in Boston. Nothing could have been more timely, for I now spent a good part of my days and not a few nights in the saddle. I was called to the most distant parts of the reservation, and had bought a fine white horse, part Arabian, which I named "Jack Frost." When I called for George to saddle him the next morning, I was surprised to have him hesitate.

"Don't you think, doctor, you had better keep pretty close to the agency until things are a little more settled?" he asked.

"Why, George, what do you mean?"

"Well, this news that the troops have been sent for, whether it is true or not, is making a good deal of talk. No telling what some fool Indian may take it into his head to do next. Some of the white employees are not stopping at the agency, they are going right on to the railroad. I heard one man say there is going to be an Injin outbreak and he intends to get out while he can."

VII. The Ghost Dance War

A religious craze such as that of 1890–91 was a thing foreign to the Indian philosophy. I recalled that a hundred years before, on the overthrow of the Algonquin nations, a somewhat similar faith was evolved by the astute Delaware prophet, brother to Tecumseh. It meant that the last hope of race entity had departed, and my people were groping blindly after spiritual relief in their bewilderment and misery. I believe that the first prophets of the "Red Christ" were innocent enough and that the people generally were sincere, but there were doubtless some who went into it for self-advertisement, and who introduced new and fantastic features to attract the crowd.

The ghost dancers had gradually concentrated on the Medicine Root creek and the edge of the "Bad Lands," and they were still further isolated by a new order from the agent, calling in all those who had not adhered to the new religion. Several thousand of these "friendlies" were soon encamped on the White Clay creek, close by the agency. It was near the middle of December, with weather unusually mild for that season. The dancers held that there would be no snow so long as their rites continued.

An Indian called Little had been guilty of some minor offense on the reservation and had hitherto evaded arrest. Suddenly he appeared at the agency on an issue day, for the express purpose, as it seemed, of defying the authorities. The assembly room of the Indian police, used also as a council room, opened out of my dispensary, and on this particular morning a council was in progress. I heard some loud talking, but was too busy to pay particular attention, though my assistant had gone in to listen to the speeches. Suddenly the place was in an uproar, and George burst into the inner office, crying excitedly "Look out for yourself, friend! They are going to fight!"

I went around to see what was going on. A crowd had gathered just outside the council room, and the police were surrounded by wild Indians with guns and drawn knives in their hands. "Hurry up with them!" one shouted, while another held his stone war-club over a policeman's head. The attempt to arrest Little had met with a stubborn resistance.

At this critical moment, a fine-looking Indian in citizen's clothes faced the excited throng, and spoke in a clear, steady, almost sarcastic voice.

"Stop! Think! What are you going to do? Kill these men of our own race? Then what? Kill all these helpless white men, women and children? And what then? What will these brave words, brave deeds lead to in the end? How long can you hold out? Your country is surrounded with a network of railroads; thousands of white soldiers will be here within three days. What ammunition have you? what provisions? What will become of your families? Think, think, my brothers! this is a child's madness."

It was the "friendly" chief, American Horse, and it seems to me as I recall the incident that this man's voice had almost magic power. It is likely that he saved us all from massacre, for the murder of the police, who represented the authority of the Government, would surely have been followed by a general massacre. It is a fact that those Indians who upheld the agent were in quite as much danger from their wilder brethren as were the whites, indeed it was said that the feeling against them was even stronger. Jack Red Cloud, son of the chief, thrust the muzzle of a cocked revolver almost into the face of American Horse. "It is you and your kind," he shouted, "who have brought us to this pass!" That brave man never flinched. Ignoring his rash accuser, he quietly reëntered the office; the door closed behind him; the mob dispersed, and for the moment the danger seemed over.

That evening I was surprised by a late call from American

Horse, the hero of the day. His wife entered close behind him. Scarcely were they seated when my door again opened softly, and Captain Sword came in, followed by Lieutenant Thunder Bear and most of the Indian police. My little room was crowded. I handed them some tobacco, which I had always at hand for my guests, although I did not smoke myself. After a silence, the chief got up and shook hands with me ceremoniously. In a short speech, he asked my advice in the difficult situation that confronted them between the ghost dancers, men of their own blood, and the Government to which they had pledged their loyalty.

Thanks to Indian etiquette, I could allow myself two or three minutes to weigh my words before replying. I finally said, in substance: "There is only one thing for us to do and be just to both sides. We must use every means for a peaceful settlement of this difficulty. Let us be patient; let us continue to reason with the wilder element, even though some hotheads may threaten our lives. If the worst happens, however, it is our solemn duty to serve the United States Government. Let no man ever say that we were disloyal! Following such a policy, dead or alive, we shall have no apology to make."

After the others had withdrawn, Sword informed me confidentially that certain young men had threatened to kill American Horse while asleep in his tent, and that his friends had prevailed upon him and his wife to ask my hospitality for a few days. I showed Mrs. American Horse to a small room that I had vacant, and soon afterward came three strokes of the office bell—the signal for me to report at the agent's office.

I found there the agent, his chief clerk, and a visiting inspector, all of whom obviously regarded the situation as serious. "You see, doctor," said the agent, "the occurrence of to-day was planned with remarkable accuracy, so that even our alert police were taken entirely by surprise and readily overpowered. What will be the sequel we can not tell, but we must be prepared for anything. I shall be glad to have your views," he added.

I told him that I still did not believe there was any widespread plot, or deliberate intention to make war upon the whites. In my own mind, I felt sure that the arrival of troops would be construed by the ghost dancers as a threat or a challenge, and would put them at once on the defensive. I was not in favor of that step; neither was Mr. Cook, who was also called into conference; but the officials evidently feared a general uprising, and argued that it was their duty to safeguard the lives of the employees and others by calling for the soldiers without more delay. Sword, Thunder Bear, and American Horse were sent for and their opinions appeared to be fully in accord with those of the agent and inspector, so the matter was given out as settled. As a matter of fact, the agent had telegraphed to Fort Robinson for troops before he made a pretense of consulting us Indians, and they were already on their way to Pine Ridge.

I scarcely knew at the time, but gradually learned afterward, that the Sioux had many grievances and causes for profound discontent, which lay back of and were more or less closely related to the ghost dance craze and the prevailing restlessness and excitement. Rations had been cut from time to time; the people were insufficiently fed, and their protests and appeals were disregarded. Never was more ruthless fraud and graft practiced upon a defenseless people than upon these poor natives by the politicians! Never were there more worthless "scraps of paper" anywhere in the world than many of the Indian treaties and Government documents! Sickness was prevalent and the death rate alarming, especially among the children. Trouble from all these causes had for some time been developing, but might have been checked by humane and conciliatory measures. The "Messiah craze" in itself was scarcely a source of danger, and one might almost as well call upon the army to suppress Billy Sunday and his hysterical followers. Other tribes than the Sioux who adopted the new religion were let alone, and the craze died a natural death in the course of a few months.

Among the leaders of the malcontents at this time were Jack Red Cloud, No Water, He Dog, Four Bears, Yellow Bear, and Kicking Bear. Friendly leaders included American Horse, Young Man Afraid of his Horses, Bad Wound, Three Stars. There was still another set whose attitude was not clearly defined, and among these men was Red Cloud, the greatest of them all. He who had led his people so brilliantly and with such

Mato-wa-nahtaka, (Kicking Bear.)
High Priest of the "Messiah Craze," 1890–91.

remarkable results, both in battle and diplomacy, was now an old man of over seventy years, living in a frame house which had been built for him within a half mile of the agency. He would come to council, but said little or nothing. No one knew exactly where he stood, but it seemed that he was broken in spirit as in body and convinced of the hopelessness of his people's cause.

It was Red Cloud who asked the historic question, at a great council held in the Black Hills region with a Government commission, and after good Bishop Whipple had finished the invocation, "Which God is our brother praying to now? Is it the same God whom they had twice deceived, when they made treaties with us which they afterward broke?"

Early in the morning after the attempted arrest of Little, George rushed into my quarters and awakened me. "Come quick!" he shouted, "the soldiers are here!" I looked along the White Clay creek toward the little railroad town of Rushville, Nebraska, twenty-five miles away, and just as the sun rose above the knife-edged ridges black with stunted pine, I perceived a moving cloud of dust that marked the trail of the Ninth Cavalry. There was instant commotion among the camps of friendly Indians. Many women and children were coming in to the agency for refuge, evidently fearing that the dreaded soldiers might attack their villages by mistake. Some who had not heard of their impending arrival hurried to the offices to ask what it meant. I assured those who appealed to me that the troops were here only to preserve order, but their suspicions were not easily allayed.

As the cavalry came nearer, we saw that they were colored troopers, wearing buffalo overcoats and muskrat caps; the Indians with their quick wit called them "buffalo soldiers." They halted, and established their temporary camp in the open space before the agency enclosure. The news had already gone out through the length and breadth of the reservation, and the wildest rumors were in circulation. Indian scouts might be seen upon every hill top, closely watching the military encampment.

At this juncture came the startling news from Fort Yates, some two hundred and fifty miles to the north of us, that Sitting Bull had been killed by Indian police while resisting arrest, and a number of his men with him, as well as several of the police. We next heard that the remnant of his band had fled in our direction, and soon afterward, that they had been joined by Big Foot's band from the western part of Cheyenne River agency, which lay directly in their road. United States troops continued to gather at strategic points, and of course the press seized upon the opportunity to enlarge upon the strained situation and predict an "Indian uprising." The reporters were among us, and managed to secure much "news" that no one else ever heard of. Border towns were fortified and cowboys and militia gathered in readiness to protect them against the "red devils." Certain classes of the frontier population industriously fomented the excitement for what there was in it for them, since much money is apt to be spent at such times. As for the poor Indians, they were quite as badly scared as the whites and perhaps with more reason.

General Brooke undertook negotiations with the ghost dancers, and finally induced them to come within reach. They camped on a flat about a mile north of us and in full view, while the more tractable bands were still gathered on the south and west. The large boarding school had locked its doors and succeeded in holding its hundreds of Indian children, partly for their own sakes, and partly as hostages for the good behavior of their fathers. At the agency were now gathered all the government employees and their families, except such as had taken flight, together with traders, missionaries, and ranchmen, army officers, and newspaper men. It was a conglomerate population.

During this time of grave anxiety and nervous tension, the cooler heads among us went about our business, and still refused to believe in the tragic possibility of an Indian war. It may be imagined that I was more than busy, though I had not such long distances to cover, for since many Indians accustomed to comfortable log houses were compelled to pass the winter in tents, there was even more sickness than usual. I had access and welcome to the camps of all the various groups and factions, a privilege shared by my good friend Father Jutz, the Catholic missionary, who was completely trusted by his people.

The Christmas season was fast approaching, and this is

perhaps the brightest spot in the mission year. The children of
the Sunday Schools, and indeed all the people, look eagerly forward to the joyous feast; barrels and boxes are received and
opened, candy bags made and filled, carols practiced, and
churches decorated with ropes of spicy evergreen.

Anxious to relieve the tension in every way within his power,
Mr. Cook and his helpers went on with their preparations upon
even a larger scale than usual. Since all of the branch stations
had been closed and the people called in, it was planned to keep
the Christmas tree standing in the chapel for a week, and to dis-
tribute gifts to a separate congregation each evening. I found
myself pressed into the service, and passed some happy hours in
the rectory. For me, at that critical time, there was inward struggle as well as the threat of outward conflict, and I could not but
recall what my "white mother" had said jokingly one day, referring to my pleasant friendships with many charming Boston
girls, "I know one Sioux who has not been conquered, and I
shall not rest till I hear of his capture!"

I had planned to enter upon my life work unhampered by any
other ties, and declared that all my love should be vested in my
people and my profession. At last, however, I had met a woman
whose sincerity was convincing and whose ideals seemed very
like my own. Her childhood had been spent almost as much out
of doors as mine, on a lonely estate high up in the Berkshire
hills; her ancestry Puritan on one side, proud Tories on the
other. She had been moved by the appeals of that wonderful
man, General Armstrong, and had gone to Hampton as a young
girl to teach the Indians there. After three years, she undertook
pioneer work in the West as teacher of a new camp school
among the wilder Sioux, and after much travel and study of their
peculiar problems had been offered the appointment she now
held. She spoke the Sioux language fluently and went among the
people with the utmost freedom and confidence. Her methods
of work were very simple and direct. I do not know what unseen
hand had guided me to her side, but on Christmas day of 1890,
Elaine Goodale and I announced our engagement.

Three days later, we learned that Big Foot's band of ghost
dancers from the Cheyenne river reservation north of us was

approaching the agency, and that Major Whiteside was in command of troops with orders to intercept them.

Late that afternoon, the Seventh Cavalry under Colonel Forsythe was called to the saddle and rode off toward Wounded Knee creek, eighteen miles away. Father Craft, a Catholic priest with some Indian blood, who knew Sitting Bull and his people, followed an hour or so later, and I was much inclined to go too, but my fiancée pointed out that my duty lay rather at home with our Indians, and I stayed.

The morning of December 29th was sunny and pleasant. We were all straining our ears toward Wounded Knee, and about the middle of the forenoon we distinctly heard the reports of the Hotchkiss guns. Two hours later, a rider was seen approaching at full speed, and in a few minutes he had dismounted from his exhausted horse and handed his message to General Brooke's orderly. The Indians were watching their own messenger, who ran on foot along the northern ridges and carried the news to the so-called "hostile" camp. It was said that he delivered his message at almost the same time as the mounted officer.

The resulting confusion and excitement was unmistakable. The white teepees disappeared as if by magic and soon the caravans were in motion, going toward the natural fortress of the "Bad Lands." In the "friendly" camp there was almost as much turmoil, and crowds of frightened women and children poured into the agency. Big Foot's band had been wiped out by the troops, and reprisals were naturally looked for. The enclosure was not barricaded in any way and we had but a small detachment of troops for our protection. Sentinels were placed, and machine guns trained on the various approaches.

A few hot-headed young braves fired on the sentinels and wounded two of them. The Indian police began to answer by shooting at several braves who were apparently about to set fire to some of the outlying buildings. Every married employee was seeking a place of safety for his family, the interpreter among them. Just then General Brooke ran out into the open, shouting at the top of his voice to the police: "Stop, stop! Doctor, tell them they must not fire until ordered!" I did so, as the bullets whistled by us, and the General's coolness perhaps saved all our lives, for we were in no position to repel a large attacking force. Since we did not reply, the scattered shots soon ceased, but the situation remained critical for several days and nights.

My office was full of refugees. I called one of my good friends aside and asked him to saddle my two horses and stay by them. "When general fighting begins, take them to Miss Goodale and see her to the railroad if you can," I told him. Then I went over to the rectory. Mrs. Cook refused to go without her husband, and Miss Goodale would not leave while there was a chance of being of service. The house was crowded with terrified people, most of them Christian Indians, whom our friends were doing their best to pacify.

At dusk, the Seventh Cavalry returned with their twenty-five dead and I believe thirty-four wounded, most of them by their own comrades, who had encircled the Indians, while few of the latter had guns. A majority of the thirty or more Indian wounded were women and children, including babies in arms. As there were not tents enough for all, Mr. Cook offered us the mission chapel, in which the Christmas tree still stood, for a temporary hospital. We tore out the pews and covered the floor with hay and quilts. There we laid the poor creatures side by side in rows, and the night was devoted to caring for them as best we could. Many were frightfully torn by pieces of shells, and the suffering was terrible. General Brooke placed me in charge and I had to do nearly all the work, for although the army surgeons were more than ready to help as soon as their own men had been cared for, the tortured Indians would scarcely allow a man in uniform to touch them. Mrs. Cook, Miss Goodale, and several of Mr. Cook's Indian helpers acted as volunteer nurses. In spite of all our efforts, we lost the greater part of them, but a few recovered, including several children who had lost all their relatives and who were adopted into kind Christian families.

On the day following the Wounded Knee massacre there was a blizzard, in the midst of which I was ordered out with several Indian police, to look for a policeman who was reported to have been wounded and left some two miles from the agency. We did not find him. This was the only time during the whole affair that I carried a weapon; a friend lent me a revolver which I put in my overcoat pocket, and it was lost on the ride. On the third day it cleared, and the ground was covered with an inch or two of fresh snow. We had feared that some of the Indian wounded might have been left on the field, and a number of us volunteered to go and see. I was placed in charge of the expedition of about a hundred civilians, ten or fifteen of whom were white men. We were supplied with wagons in which to convey any whom we might find still alive. Of course a photographer and several reporters were of the party.

Fully three miles from the scene of the massacre we found the body of a woman completely covered with a blanket of snow, and from this point on we found them scattered along as they had been relentlessly hunted down and slaughtered while fleeing for their lives. Some of our people discovered relatives or friends among the dead, and there was much wailing and mourning. When we reached the spot where the Indian camp had stood, among the fragments of burned tents and other belongings we saw the frozen bodies lying close together or piled one upon another. I counted eighty bodies of men who had been in the council and who were almost as helpless as the women and babes when the deadly fire began, for nearly all their guns had been taken from them. A reckless and desperate young Indian fired the first shot when the search for weapons was well under way, and immediately the troops opened fire from all sides, killing not only unarmed men, women, and children, but their own comrades who stood opposite them, for the camp was entirely surrounded.

It took all of my nerve to keep my composure in the face of this spectacle, and of the excitement and grief of my Indian companions, nearly every one of whom was crying aloud or singing his death song. The white men became very nervous, but I set them to examining and uncovering every body to see if one were living. Although they had been lying untended in the snow and cold for two days and nights, a number had survived. Among them I found a baby of about a year old warmly wrapped and entirely unhurt. I brought her in, and she was afterward adopted and educated by an army officer. One man who was severely wounded begged me to fill his pipe. When we brought him into the chapel he was welcomed by his wife and daughters with cries of joy, but he died a day or two later.

Under a wagon I discovered an old woman, totally blind and entirely helpless. A few had managed to crawl away to some place of shelter, and we found in a log store near by several who were badly hurt and others who had died after reaching there. After we had dispatched several wagon loads to the agency, we observed groups of warriors watching us from adjacent buttes; probably friends of the victims who had come there for the same purpose as ourselves. A majority of our party, fearing an attack, insisted that some one ride back to the agency for an escort of soldiers, and as mine was the best horse, it fell to me to go. I covered the eighteen miles in quick time and was not interfered with in any way, although if the Indians had meant mischief they could easily have picked me off from any of the ravines and gulches.

All this was a severe ordeal for one who had so lately put all his faith in the Christian love and lofty ideals of the white man. Yet I passed no hasty judgment, and was thankful that I might be of some service and relieve even a small part of the suffering. An appeal published in a Boston paper brought us liberal supplies of much needed clothing, and linen for dressings. We worked on. Bishop Hare of South Dakota visited us, and was overcome by faintness when he entered his mission chapel, thus transformed into a rude hospital.

After some days of extreme tension, and weeks of anxiety, the "hostiles," so called, were at last induced to come in and submit to a general disarmament. Father Jutz, the Catholic missionary, had gone bravely among them and used all his influence toward a peaceful settlement. The troops were all recalled and took part in a grand review before General Miles, no doubt intended to impress the Indians with their superior force.

In March, all being quiet, Miss Goodale decided to send in her resignation and go East to visit her relatives, and our wedding day was set for the following June.

VIII. War with the Politicians

When the most industrious and advanced Indians on the reservation, to the number of thousands, were ordered into camp within gunshot of Pine Ridge agency, they had necessarily left their homes, their live stock, and most of their household belongings unguarded. In all troubles between the two races, history tells us that the innocent and faithful Indians have been sufferers, and this case was no exception. There was much sickness from exposure, and much unavoidable sorrow and anxiety. Furthermore, the "war" being over, these loyal Indians found that their houses had been entered and pillaged, and many of their cattle and horses had disappeared.

The authorities laid all this to the door of the "hostiles," and no doubt in some cases the charge may have been true. On the other hand, this was a golden opportunity for white horse and cattle thieves in the surrounding country, and the ranch owners within a radius of a hundred miles claimed large losses also. Moreover, the Government herd of "issue cattle" was found to be greatly depleted. It was admitted that some had been killed for food by those Indians who fled in terror to the "Bad Lands," but only a limited number could be accounted for in this way, and little of the stolen property was ever found. An inspector was ordered to examine and record these "depredation claims," and Congress passed a special appropriation of one hundred thousand dollars to pay them. We shall hear more of this later.

I have tried to make it clear that there was no "Indian outbreak" in 1890–91, and that such trouble as we had may justly be charged to the dishonest politicians, who through unfit

67

appointees first robbed the Indians, then bullied them, and finally in a panic called for troops to suppress them. From my first days at Pine Ridge, certain Indians and white people had taken every occasion to whisper into my reluctant ears the tale of wrongs, real or fancied, committed by responsible officials on the reservation, or by their connivance. To me these stories were unbelievable, from the point of view of common decency. I held that a great government such as ours would never condone or permit any such practices, while administering large trust funds and standing in the relation of guardian to a race made helpless by lack of education and of legal safeguards. At that time, I had not dreamed what American politics really is, and I had the most exalted admiration for our noted public men. Accordingly, I dismissed these reports as mere gossip or the inventions of mischief-makers.

In March of 1891 I was invited to address the Congregational Club of Chicago, and on my arrival in the city I found to my surprise that the press still fostered the illusion of a general Indian uprising in the spring. It was reported that all the towns adjoining the Sioux reservations had organized and were regularly drilling a home guard for their protection. These alarmists seemed either ignorant or forgetful of the fact that there were only about thirty thousand Sioux altogether, or perhaps six thousand men of fighting age, more than half of whom had been civilized and Christianized for a generation and had just proved their loyalty and steadfastness through a trying time. Furthermore, the leaders of the late "hostiles" were even then in confinement in Fort Sheridan. When I was approached by the reporters, I reminded them of this, and said that everything was quiet in the field, but if there were any danger from the ghost dancers, Chicago was in the most immediate peril!

Fortunately we had in the office of Commissioner of Indian Affairs at that time a sincere man, and one who was deeply in sympathy with educational and missionary work, General Morgan of Indiana. He was a lover of fair play, and throughout my fight for justice he gave me all the support within his power. As I have before intimated, I found at Pine Ridge no conveyance for the doctor's professional use, and indeed no medical equipment worthy the name. The agency doctor was thrown entirely upon his own resources, without the support of colleagues, and there was no serious attempt at sanitation or preventive work. I had spent a good part of my salary, as well as funds contributed by friends for the purpose, in the purchase of suitable medical supplies and instruments. Finally, I boldly asked for a team and buggy, also a hospital for critical cases, with a trained nurse, and a house for us to live in. Somewhat to my surprise, all of these were allowed. I was ambitious to give efficient service, so far as it was possible, and I loved my work, though the field was too large and the sick were too many for one man to care for, and there were many obstacles in the way. One was the native prejudice, still strong, against the white man's medicine, and especially against any kind of surgical operation. The people were afraid of anæsthesia, and even in cases where life depended upon it, they had steadfastly refused to allow a limb to be amputated. If I so much as put on a plaster cast, I had no sooner left our temporary hospital than they took it off.

It may be of interest to tell how this prejudice was in part overcome. One day my friend Three Stars, a Christian chief, came in with his wife, who had dislocated her shoulder. "Can you help her?" he asked. "Yes," I said, "but I must first put her to sleep. You should have brought her to me last night, when it first happened," I added, "and then that would not have been necessary."

"You know best," replied Three Stars, "I leave it entirely with you." In the presence of a number of the wounded Indians, I administered a small quantity of chloroform and jerked the arm back into its socket. She came back to consciousness laughing. It appeared to them a miracle, and I was appealed to after that whenever I dressed a painful wound, to "give me some of that stuff you gave to Three Stars' wife."

Not long afterwards, I amputated the leg of a mixed blood, which had been terribly crushed, and he not only recovered perfectly but was soon able to get about with ease on the artificial limb that I procured for him. My reputation was now established. I had gained much valuable experience, and in this connection I want to express my appreciation of the kindness of several army surgeons with whom it was my pleasure to work, one of whom took my place during a six weeks' leave of absence, when I went east to be married.

I had some interesting experiences with the Indian conjurers, or "medicine men," to use the names commonly given. I would rather say, mental healer or Christian scientist of our day, for the medicine man was all of that, and further he practised massage or osteopathy, used the Turkish bath, and some useful vegetable remedies. But his main hold on the minds of the people was gained through his appeals to the spirits and his magnetic and hypnotic powers.

I was warned that these men would seriously hamper my work, but I succeeded in avoiding antagonism by a policy of friendliness. Even when brought face to face with them in the homes of my patients, I preserved a professional and brotherly attitude. I recall one occasion when a misunderstanding between the parents of a sick child had resulted in a double call. The father, who was a policeman and a good friend of mine, urgently requested me to see his child; while the frantic mother sent for the most noted of the medicine men.

"Brother," I said, when I found him already in attendance, "I am glad you got here first. I had a long way to come, and the children need immediate attention."

"I think so too," he replied, "but now that you are here, I will withdraw."

"Why so? Surely two doctors should be better than one," I retorted. "Let us consult together. In the first place, we must determine what ails the child. Then we will decide upon the treatment." He seemed pleased, and I followed up the suggestion of a consultation by offering to enter with him the sweat bath he had prepared as a means of purification before beginning his work. After that, I had no difficulty in getting his consent to my treatment of the patient, and in time he became one of my warm friends. It was not unusual for him and other conjurers to call at my office to consult me, or "borrow" my medicine.

I had some of the wounded in my care all winter. I remember

one fine looking man who was severely injured; a man of ordinary strength would have succumbed, but his strength and courage were exceptional, and best of all, he had perfect faith in my ability to restore him to health. All through those months of trial, his pretty young wife was my faithful assistant. Every morning she came to see him with her baby on her back, cheering him and inspiring us both to do our best. When at last he was able to travel, they came together to say good-bye. She handed me something, carefully wrapped in paper, and asked me not to open it until they had gone. When I did so, I found that she had cut off her beautiful long braids of hair and given them to me in token of her gratitude!

I was touched by this little illustration of woman's devotion, and happy in the thought that I was soon to realize my long dream—to become a complete man! I thought of little else than the good we two could do together, and was perfectly contented with my salary of twelve hundred dollars a year. In spite of all that I had gone through, life was not yet a serious matter to me. I had faith in every one, and accepted civilization and Christianity at their face value—a great mistake, as I was to learn later on. I had come back to my people, not to minister to their physical needs alone, but to be a missionary in every sense of the word, and as I was much struck with the loss of manliness and independence in these, the first "reservation Indians" I had ever known, I longed above all things to help them to regain their self-respect.

On June 18, 1891, I was married to Elaine Goodale in the Church of the Ascension, New York City, by the Rev. Dr. Donald. Her two sisters were bridesmaids, and I had my chum in the medical school for best man, and two Dartmouth classmates as ushers. Many well known people were present. After the wedding breakfast in her father's apartments, we went to "Sky Farm," my wife's birth-place in the beautiful Berkshire hills, where she and her sister Dora, as little girls, wrote the "Apple Blossoms" and other poems. A reception was given for us at Dorchester by Mr. and Mrs. Wood, and after attending the Wellesley College commencement, and spending a few days with my wife's family, we returned to the West by way of

Montreal. At Flandreau, South Dakota, my brother John had gathered all the family and the whole band of Flandreau Sioux to welcome us. There my father had brought me home from Canada, an absolute wild Indian, only eighteen years earlier! My honored father had been dead for some years, but my brothers had arranged to have a handsome memorial to him erected and unveiled at that time.

Our new home was building when we reached Pine Ridge, and we started life together in the old barracks, while planning the finishing and furnishing of the new. It was ready for us early in the fall. I had gained permission to add an open fireplace and a few other homelike touches at my own expense. We had the chiefs and leading men to dine with us, and quite as often some of the humbler Indians and poor old women were our guests. In fact, we kept open house, and the people loved to come and talk with us in their own tongue. My wife accompanied me on many of my trips now that I had a carriage, and was always prepared with clean clothing, bandages, and nourishing food for my needy patients.

There was nothing I called my own save my dogs and horses and my medicine bags, yet I was perfectly happy, for I had not only gained the confidence of my people, but that of the white residents, and even the border ranchmen called me in now and then. I answered every call, and have ridden forty or fifty miles in a blizzard, over dangerous roads, sometimes at night, while my young wife suffered much more than I in the anxiety with which she awaited my return. That was a bitterly cold winter, I remember, and we had only wood fires (soft wood) and no "modern conveniences"; yet we kept in perfect health. The year rolled around and our first child was born—a little girl whom we called Dora.

Meanwhile, though the troops had been recalled, we were under military agents; there were several changes, and our relations were pleasant with them all. The time came for the small annual payment of treaty money, and the one hundred thousand dollar payment for depredation claims, of which I have spoken, was also to be made by a special disbursing agent. This payment was not made by check, as usual, but in cash, and I was asked to

ELAINE GOODALE EASTMAN.

be one of the three witnesses. I told the special agent that, as I was almost constantly occupied, it would be impossible for me to witness the payment, which would take several days; but he assured me that if only one of the three were present at a time it would be sufficient, and, understanding my duties to be only nominal, I consented.

I was in the office from time to time while the payment was going on, and saw the people sign their names, generally by mark, on the roll which had been prepared, opposite the amount which each was supposed to receive; then a clerk at another desk handed each in turn a handful of silver and bills, and he passed out as quickly as possible. The money was not counted out to him, and he was given no chance to count it until he got outside. Even then, many could not count it, and did not clearly understand how much it ought to be, while the traders and others were close at hand to get all or part of it without delay.

Before I knew it, I was approached by one and another, who declared that they had not received the full amount, and I found that in numerous cases reliable persons had counted the cash as soon as the payees came out of the office. A very able white teacher, a college graduate, counted for several old people who were protégés of hers; an influential native minister did the same, and so did several others; all reported that the amount was short from ten to fifteen per cent. When any one brought a shortage to the attention of the disbursing agent or his clerk, he was curtly told that he had made a mistake or lost some of the money.

The complaints grew louder, and other suspicious circumstances were reported. Within a few days it was declared that an investigation would be ordered. The agent who had made the payment and immediately left the agency, being informed of the situation, came back and tried to procure affidavits to show that it had been an honest payment. He urged me to sign, as one of the original witnesses, arguing that I had already committed myself. I refused. I said, "After all, I did not see the full amount paid to each claimant. As the payment was conducted, it was impossible for me to do so. I trusted you, therefore I allowed you to use my name, but I don't care to sign again."

The regular agent in charge of our Indians at the time was, as I have said, an army officer, with military ideas of discipline. Like myself, he had been in the field much of the time while the payment was going on, but had officially vouched for its correctness and signed all the papers, and he took his stand upon this. He remonstrated with me for my position in the matter, and did his best to avoid an investigation; but I was convinced that a gross fraud had been committed, and in my inexperience I believed that it had only to be exposed to be corrected. I determined to do all in my power to secure justice for those poor, helpless people, even though it must appear that I was careless in signing the original papers.

I added my protest to that of others, and the department sent out a Quaker, an inspector whose record was excellent and who went about the work in a direct and straightforward way. He engaged a reliable interpreter, and called in witnesses on both sides. At the end of a fortnight, he reported that about ten thousand dollars had been dishonestly withheld from the Indians. A few of the better educated and more influential, especially mixed bloods, had been paid in full, while the old and ignorant had lost as high as fifteen or twenty per cent of their money. Evidence in support of this decision was sent to Washington.

After a short interval, I learned with astonishment that the report of this trusted inspector had not been accepted by the Secretary of the Interior, who had ordered a second investigation to supersede the first. Naturally, the second investigation was a farce and quickly ended in "white-washing" the special payment. The next step was to punish those who had testified for the Indians or tried to bring about an honest investigation in the face of official opposition. Of these, I had been perhaps the most active and outspoken.

The usual method of disciplining agency Indians in such a case is to deprive them of various privileges, possibly of rations also, and sometimes to imprison them on trivial pretexts. White men with Indian wives, and missionaries, may be ordered off the reservation as "disturbers of the peace," while with Government employees, some grounds are usually found for their dismissal from the service.

I was promptly charged with "insubordination" and other things, but my good friend, General Morgan, then Commissioner, declined to entertain the charges, and I, on my part, kept up the fight at Washington through influential friends, and made every effort to prove my case, or rather, the case of the people, for I had at no time any personal interest in the payment. The local authorities followed the usual tactics, and undertook to force a resignation by making my position at Pine Ridge intolerable. An Indian agent has almost autocratic power, and the conditions of life on an agency are such as to make every resident largely dependent upon his good will. We soon found ourselves hampered in our work and harassed by every imaginable annoyance. My requisitions were overlooked or "forgotten," and it became difficult to secure the necessaries of life. I would receive a curt written order to proceed without delay to some remote point to visit a certain alleged patient; then, before I had covered the distance, would be overtaken by a mounted policeman with arbitrary orders to return at once to the agency. On driving in rapidly and reporting to the agent's office for details of the supposed emergency, I might be rebuked for overdriving the horses, and charged with neglect of some chronic case of which I had either never been informed, or to which it had been physically impossible for me to give regular attention.

This sort of thing went on for several months, and I was finally summoned to Washington for a personal conference. I think I may safely say that my story was believed by Senators Dawes and Hoar, and by Commissioner Morgan also. I saw the Secretary of the Interior and the President, but they were noncommittal. On my return, the same inspector who had whitewashed the payment was directed to investigate the "strained relations" between the agent and myself, and my wife, who had meantime published several very frank letters in influential eastern papers, was made a party in the case.

I will not dwell upon the farcical nature of this "investigation." The inspector was almost openly against us from the start, and the upshot of the affair was that I was shortly offered a transfer. The agent could not be dislodged, and my position had become impossible. The superintendent of the boarding school, a cler-

gyman, and one or two others who had fought on our side were
also forced to leave. We had many other warm sympathizers
who could not speak out without risking their livelihood.

We declined to accept the compromise, being utterly disillu-
sioned and disgusted with these revelations of Government mis-
management in the field, and realizing the helplessness of the
best-equipped Indians to secure a fair deal for their people.
Later experience, both my own and that of others, has confirmed me in this view. Had it not been for strong friends in the
East and on the press, and the unusual boldness and disregard
of personal considerations with which we had conducted the
fight, I could not have lasted a month. All other means failing,
these men will not hesitate to manufacture evidence against a
man's, or a woman's, personal reputation in order to attain their
ends.

It was a great disappointment to us both to give up our plans
of work and our first home, to which we had devoted much lov-
ing thought and most of our little means; but it seemed to us
then the only thing to do. We had not the heart to begin the
same thing over again elsewhere. I resigned my position in the
Indian service, and removed with my family to the city of St.
Paul, where I proposed to enter upon the independent practice
of medicine.

IX. Civilization as Preached and Practised

A fter thirty years of exile from the land of my nativity and the home of my ancestors, I came back to Minnesota in 1893. My mother was born on the shores of Lake Harriet; my great-grandfather's village is now a part of the beautiful park system of the city of Minneapolis.

I came to St. Paul with very little money, for one can not save much out of one hundred dollars a month, and we had been compelled to sacrifice nearly all that we had spent on our little home. It was midwinter, and our baby daughter was only eight months old; but our courage was good nevertheless. I had to wait for the regular state medical examination before being admitted to practice, as Minnesota was one of the first states to pass such a law, and the examinations were searching and covered three days' time. If I remember rightly, there were some forty-five applicants who took them with me, and I was told that nearly half of them failed to pass. It was especially hard on country practitioners who had practised successfully for many years, but were weak in theory of medicine along certain lines.

Although a young couple in a strange city, we were cordially received socially, and while seriously handicapped by lack of means, we had determined to win out. I opened an office, hung out my sign, and waited for patients. It was the hardest work I had ever done! Most of the time we were forced to board for the sake of economy, and were hard put to it to meet office rent and our modest living expenses. At this period I was peculiarly tried with various temptations, by yielding to which it seemed that I could easily relieve myself from financial strain. I was persistently solicited for illegal practice, and this by persons who were not only intelligent, but apparently of good social standing. In their fear of exposure, they were ready to go to large expense, and were astonished when I refused to consider anything of the sort. A large number came to me for Indian medicine and treatment. I told them, of course, that I had no such medicine. Again, one of the best known "doctors" of this class in the Northwest invited me to go into partnership with him. Finally, a prominent business man of St. Paul offered to back me up financially if I would put up an "Indian medicine" under my own name, assuring me that there was "a fortune in it."

To be sure, I had been bitterly disappointed in the character of the United States army and the honor of Government officials. Still, I had seen the better side of civilization, and I determined that the good men and women who had helped me should not be betrayed. The Christ ideal might be radical, visionary, even impractical, as judged in the light of my later experiences; it still seemed to me logical, and in line with most of my Indian training. My heart was still strong, and I had the continual inspiration of a brave comrade at my side.

With all the rest, I was deeply regretful of the work that I had left behind. I could not help thinking that if the President knew, if the good people of this country knew, of the wrong, it would yet be righted. I had not seen half of the savagery of civilization! While I had plenty of leisure, I began to put upon paper some of my earliest recollections, with the thought that our children might some day like to read of that wilderness life. When my wife discovered what I had written, she insisted upon sending it to *St. Nicholas.* Much to my surprise, the sketches were immediately accepted and appeared during the following year. This was the beginning of my first book, "Indian Boyhood," which was not completed until several years later.

We were slowly gaining ground, when one day a stranger called on me in my office. He was, I learned, one of the field secretaries of the International Committee of Y.M.C.A., and had apparently called to discuss the feasibility of extending this movement among the Indians. After we had talked for some time, he broached the plan of putting a man into the Indian field, and ended by urging me to consider taking up the work. My first thought was that it was out of the question to sacrifice my profession and practice at this juncture, when I was just getting a promising start. Then, too, I doubted my fitness for religious work. He still pressed me to accept, pointing out the far-reaching importance of this new step, and declared that they had not been able to hear of any one else of my race so well fitted to undertake it. We took the matter under consideration, and with some reluctance I agreed to organize the field if they would meantime educate a young Indian whom I would name to be my successor. I had in mind the thought that, when the man I had chosen should be graduated from the International Training School at Springfield, Massachusetts, I could again return to my practice.

I selected Arthur Tibbetts, a Sioux, who was duly graduated in three years, when I resigned in his favor. I had been unable to keep an office in St. Paul, where we made our home, but I carried my small medical case with me on all my trips, and was often appealed to by the Indians for my professional help. I traveled over a large part of the western states and in Canada, visiting the mission stations among Indians of all tribes, and organizing young men's associations wherever conditions permitted. I think I organized some forty-three associations. This gave me a fine opportunity to study Protestant missionary effort among Indians. I seriously considered the racial attitude toward God, and almost unconsciously reopened the book of my early religious training, asking myself how it was that our simple lives were so imbued with the spirit of worship, while much church-going among white and nominally Christian Indians led often to such very small results.

A new point of view came to me then and there. This latter was a machine-made religion. It was supported by money, and more money could only be asked for on the showing made; therefore too many of the workers were after quantity rather than quality of religious experience.

I was constantly meeting with groups of young men of the Sioux, Cheyennes, Crees, Ojibways, and others, in log cabins or little frame chapels, and trying to set before them in simple language the life and character of the Man Jesus. I was cordially received everywhere, and always listened to with the closest attention. Curiously enough, even among these men who were seeking light on the white man's ideals, the racial philosophy emerged from time to time.

I remember one old battle-scarred warrior who sat among the young men got up and said, in substance: "Why, we have followed this law you speak of for untold ages! We owned nothing, because everything is from Him. Food was free, land free as sunshine and rain. Who has changed all this? The white man; and yet he says he is a believer in God! He does not seem to inherit any of the traits of his Father, nor does he follow the example set by his brother Christ."

Another of the older men had attentively followed our Bible study and attended every meeting for a whole week. I finally called upon him for his views. After a long silence, he said:

"I have come to the conclusion that this Jesus was an Indian. He was opposed to material acquirement and to great possessions. He was inclined to peace. He was as unpractical as any Indian and set no price upon his labor of love. These are not the principles upon which the white man has founded his civilization. It is strange that he could not rise to these simple principles which were commonly observed among our people."

These words put the spell of an uncomfortable silence upon our company, but it did not appear that the old man had intended any sarcasm or unkindness, for after a minute he added that he was glad we had selected such an unusual character for our model.

At the Crow agency I met a Scotchman, a missionary of fine type, who was doing good work. This man told me a strange story of his conversion. As a young man, he had traveled extensively in this and other countries. He spent one winter at Manitoba, near an Indian reservation, and there he met a young Indian who had been converted by one of his own tribesmen, and was intensely interested in the life of Christ. This young man was a constant reader in his Indian Bible, and he talked of Christ so eloquently and so movingly as to cause serious thought on the part of the traveler. To make a long story short, he finally went home to Scotland and studied for the ministry, and then returned to America to enter the field of Indian missions. It happened that the young Indian who made so deep an impression on his white friend was my own uncle, who had been baptized Joseph Eastman.

My two uncles who were in the Custer fight lived in Canada from the time of our flight in 1862, and both died there. I was happy to be sent to that part of the country in time to see the elder one alive. He had been a father to me up to the age of fifteen, and I had not seen him for over twenty years. I found him a farmer, living in a Christian community. I had sent word in advance of my coming, and my uncle's family had made of it a great occasion. All of my old playmates were there. My uncle was so happy that tears welled up in his eyes. "When we are old," he smiled, "our hearts are not strong in moments like this. The Great Spirit has been kind to let me see my boy again before I die." The early days were recalled as we feasted together, and all agreed that the chances were I should have been killed before reaching the age of twenty, if I had remained among them; for, said they, I was very anxious to emulate my uncle, who had been a warrior of great reputation. Afterward I visited the grave of my grandmother, whose devotion had meant so much to me as a motherless child. This was one of the great moments of my life.

Throughout this period of my work I was happy, being unhampered by official red tape in the effort to improve conditions among my people. The Superintendent of Indian Affairs in Manitoba was very kind and gave me every facility to go among the Indians. He asked me to make a comparative report on their condition on both sides of the border, but this I declined to undertake, unwilling to prejudice the Government officials under whom I must carry on my work in the United States.

Another trip took me among the Ojibways, who used to take many a Sioux scalp, while we prized an eagle feather earned in battle with them. But those who had actually engaged in warlike exploits were now old and much inclined toward a peaceful life. I met some very able native preachers among them. I also visited for the first time the "Five Civilized Tribes" of the Indian Territory, now the state of Oklahoma. As is well known, these people intermarried largely among the whites, and had their own governments, schools, and thriving towns. When I appeared at Tahlequah, the Cherokee capital, the Senate took a recess in honor of their Sioux visitor. At Bacone College I addressed the students, and at the Cherokee male and female seminaries. It was an odd coincidence that at the latter school I found one of the young ladies in the act of reading an essay on my wife, Elaine Goodale Eastman!

Among other duties of my position, I was expected to make occasional speaking trips through the East to arouse interest in the work, and it thus happened that I addressed large audiences in Chicago, New York, Boston, and at Lake Mohonk. I was taken by slum and settlement workers to visit the slums and dives of the cities, which gave another shock to my ideals of "Christian civilization." Of course, I had seen something of the poorer parts of Boston during my medical course, but not at night, and not in a way to realize the horror and wretchedness of it as I did now. To be sure, I had been taught even as a child that there are always some evil minded men in every nation, and we knew well what it is to endure physical hardship, but our poor lost nothing of their self-respect and dignity. Our great men not only divided their last kettle of food with a neighbor, but if great grief should come to them, such as the death of child or wife, they would voluntarily give away their few possessions and begin life over again in token of their sorrow. We could not conceive of the extremes of luxury and misery existing thus side by side, for it was common observation with us that the coarse weeds, if permitted to grow, will choke out the more delicate flowers. These things troubled me very much; yet I still held before my race the highest, and as yet unattained, ideals of the white man.

One of the strongest rebukes I ever received from an Indian for my acceptance of these ideals and philosophy was administered by an old chief of the Sac and Fox tribe in Iowa. I was invited to visit them by the churches of Toledo and Tama City, which were much concerned by the absolute refusal of this small tribe to accept civilization and Christianity. I surmise that these good people hoped to use me as an example of the benefits of education for the Indian.

I was kindly received at their village, and made, as I thought, a pretty good speech, emphasizing the necessity of educating their children, and urging their acceptance of the Christian religion. The old chief rose to answer. He was glad that I had come to visit them. He was also glad that I was apparently satisfied with the white man's religion and his civilization. As for them, he said, neither of these had seemed good to them. The white man had showed neither respect for nature nor reverence toward God, but, he thought, tried to buy God with the by-products of nature. He tried to buy his way into heaven, but he did not even know where heaven is.

"As for us," he concluded, "we shall still follow the old trail. If you should live long, and some day the Great Spirit shall permit you to visit us again, you will find us still Indians, eating with wooden spoons out of bowls of wood. I have done."

I was even more impressed a few minutes later, when one of his people handed me my pocket book containing my railway tickets and a considerable sum of money. I had not even missed it! I said to the state missionary who was at my side, "Better let these Indians alone! If I had lost my money in the streets of your Christian city, I should probably have never seen it again."

My effort was to make the Indian feel that Christianity is not at fault for the white man's sins, but rather the lack of it, and I freely admitted that this nation is not Christian, but declared that the Christians in it are trying to make it so. I found the facts and the logic of them often hard to dispute, but was partly consoled by the wonderful opportunity to come into close contact with the racial mind, and to refresh my understanding of the philosophy in which I had been trained, but which had been overlaid and superseded by a college education. I do not know how much good I accomplished, but I did my best.

X. At the Nation's Capital

My work for the International Committee of Young Men's Christian Associations brought me into close association with some of the best products of American civilization. I believe that such men as Richard Morse, John R. Mott, Wilbur Messer, Charles Ober and his brother, and others, have through their organization and personal influence contributed vitally to the stability and well-being of the nation. Among the men on the International Committee whom I met at this time and who gave me a strong impression of what they stood for, were Colonel John J. McCook, David Murray, Thomas Cochrane, and Cornelius Vanderbilt. I have said some hard things of American Christianity, but in these I referred to the nation as a whole and to the majority of its people, not to individual Christians. Had I not known some such, I should long ago have gone back to the woods.

I wished very much to resume my profession of medicine, but I was as far as ever from having the capital for a start, and we had now three children. At this juncture, I was confronted by what seemed a hopeful opportunity. Some of the leading men of the Sioux, among them my own brother, Rev. John Eastman, came to me for a consultation. They argued that I was the man of their tribe best fitted to look after their interests at Washington. They had begun to realize that certain of these interests were of great importance, involving millions of dollars. Although not a lawyer, they gave me power of attorney to act for them in behalf of these claims, and to appear as their representative before the Indian Bureau, the President, and Congress.

After signing the necessary papers, I went to Washington, where I urged our rights throughout two sessions and most of a third, while during the summers I still traveled among the Sioux. I learned that scarcely one of our treaties with the United States had been carried out in good faith in all of its provisions. After the early friendship treaties which involved no cession of land, the first was signed in 1824. By this agreement the Sioux gave up a long strip of land lying along the west bank of the Mississippi, and including some of northern Missouri and eastern Iowa. Out of the proceeds, we paid several thousand dollars to the Iowa and Otoe Indians who inhabited this country conjointly with us. Next came the treaty ratified in 1837, by which we parted with all the territory lying in the southern part of Wisconsin, southeastern Minnesota, and northeastern Iowa. For this vast domain the Government gave us a few thousand dollars in money and goods, together with many promises, and established for us a trust fund of three hundred thousand dollars, upon which interest at five per cent was to be paid "forever." This treaty affected only certain bands of the Sioux.

In 1851, we ceded another large tract in Iowa and Minnesota, including some of the best agricultural lands in the United States, and for this we were to receive ten cents an acre. Two large trust funds were established for the four bands interested, on which interest at five per cent was to be paid annually for fifty years. In addition, the Government agreed to furnish schools, farmers, blacksmith shops, etc. for the civilization of the Sioux. Only nine annual payments had been made when there was failure to meet them for two successive years. Much of our game had disappeared; the people were starving; and this state of affairs, together with other frauds on the part of Government officials and Indian traders, brought on the frightful "Minnesota massacre" in 1862. After this tragedy, many of the Sioux fled into Canada, and the remnant were moved out of the state and on to a new reservation in Nebraska. Furthermore, the remaining annuities due them under the treaty were arbitrarily confiscated as a "punishment" for the uprising. It was the claim for these lost annuities, in particular, together with some minor

OHIYESA THE SECOND, AT FIVE YEARS OF AGE, 1903.

matters, that the Indians now desired to have adjusted, and for which they sent me to the capital.

Now for the first time I seriously studied the machinery of government, and before I knew it, I was a lobbyist. I came to Washington with a great respect for our public men and institutions. Although I had had some disillusionizing experiences with the lower type of political henchmen on the reservations, I reasoned that it was because they were almost beyond the pale of civilization and clothed with supreme authority over a helpless and ignorant people, that they dared do the things they did. Under the very eye of the law and of society, I thought, this could scarcely be tolerated. I was confident that a fair hearing would be granted, and our wrongs corrected without undue delay. I had overmuch faith in the civilized ideal, and I was again disappointed.

I made up my mind at the start that I would keep aloof from the shyster lawyers, and indeed I did not expect to need any legal help until the matter should come before the Court of Claims, which could not be until Congress had acted upon it.

At that time—and I am told that it is much the same now—an Indian could not do business with the Department through his attorney. The officials received me courteously enough, and assured me that the matters I spoke of should be attended to, but as soon as my back was turned, they pigeon-holed them. After waiting patiently, I would resort to the plan of getting one of the Massachusetts Senators, who were my friends, to ask for the papers in the case, and this was generally effective. The Bureau chiefs soon learned that I had studied our treaty agreements and had some ground for any request that I might make. Naturally enough, every Northwestern Indian who came to Washington desired to consult me, and many of them had come on account of personal grievances which I could not take up. Complaints of every description came to my ear, not from Indians alone, as some were from earnest white men and women who had served among the Indians and had come up against official graft or abuses. I could not help them much, and had to stick pretty closely to my main business.

I was soon haunted and pestered by minor politicians and

grafters, each of whom claimed that he was the right-hand man of this or that congressman, and that my measure could not pass unless I had the vote of "his" man. Of course, he expected something in exchange for that vote, or rather the promise of it. Armed with a letter of introduction from one of my staunch eastern senatorial friends, I would approach a legislator who was a stranger to me, in the hope of being allowed to explain to him the purport of our measure. He would listen a while and perhaps refer me to some one else. I would call on the man he named, and to my disgust be met with a demand for a liberal percentage on the whole amount to be recovered. If I refused to listen to this proposal, I would soon find the legislator in question "drumming up" some objection to the bill, and these tactics would be kept up until we yielded, or made some sort of compromise. My brother John was with me in this work. He is a fine character-reader, and would often say to me on leaving some one's office, "Do not trust that man; he is dishonest; he will not keep his word." I found after many months of effort, that political and personal feuds in Congress persistently delayed measures which I had looked upon as only common justice; and two of the injured bands have not received their dues to this day.

I appeared from time to time before both House and Senate committees on Indian Affairs, and a few cases I carried to the President. In this way I have had personal relations with four Presidents of the United States, Harrison, Cleveland, McKinley, and Roosevelt. At one time I appeared before the committee of which Senator Allison of Iowa was chairman, on the question of allowing the Sisseton Sioux the privilege of leasing their unused allotments to neighboring farmers, without first referring the agreements to the Secretary of the Interior. The point of the request was that the red tape and long delays that seem to be inseparable from the system, greatly handicapped friendly and honest white farmers in their dealings with the Indians, and, as a result, much land lay idle and unbroken.

Some one had circulated a rumor that this measure was fathered by one of the South Dakota senators, with the object of securing some fine Indian lands for his constituents. As soon as

I heard of this, I asked for a hearing, which was granted, and I told the committee that this was the Indians' own bill. "We desire to learn business methods," I said, "and we can only do this by handling our own property. You learn by experience to manage your business. How are we Indians to learn if you take from us the wisdom that is born of mistakes, and leave us to suffer the stings of robbery and deception, with no opportunity to guard against its recurrence? I know that some will misuse this privilege, and some will be defrauded, but the experiment will be worth all it costs." Instead of asking me further questions upon the bill, they asked: "Where did you go to school? Why are there not more Indians like you?"

As I have said, nearly every Indian delegation that came to the capital in those days—and they were many—appealed to me for advice, and often had me go over their business with them before presenting it. I was sometimes with them when they had secured their hearing before the Indian Commissioner or the committees of Congress, and in this way I heard some interesting speeches. The Ojibways have much valuable pine land, aggregating millions of dollars. Congress had passed an act authorizing a special commissioner to dispose of the lumber for the Indians' benefit, but the new man had not been long in office when it appeared that he was in with large lumber interests. There was general complaint, but as usual, the Indians were only laughed at, for the official was well entrenched behind the influence of the lumber kings, and of his political party.

At last the Ojibways succeeded in bringing the matter before the House committee on Indian affairs, of which James Sherman of New York was chairman. The chief of the delegation addressed the committee somewhat as follows:

"You are very wise men, since to you this great nation entrusts the duty of making laws for the whole people. Because of this, we have trusted you, and have hitherto respected the men whom you have sent to manage our affairs. You recently sent one who was formerly of your number to sell our pines, and he is paid with our money, ten thousand dollars a year. It has been proved that he receives money from the lumber men. He has been underselling all others. We pray you take him away! Every day that you allow him to stay, much money melts away, and great forests fall in thunder!"

Many good speeches lost their effect because of the failure of the uneducated interpreter to render them intelligently, but in this instance a fine linguist interpreted for the chief, the Rev. James Gilfillan, for many years an Episcopal missionary among the Ojibways and well acquainted with their language and ways.

The old men often amused me by their shrewd comments upon our public men. "Old Tom" Beveredge was the Indians' hotel-keeper. They all knew him, and his house was the regular rendezvous. Some Sioux chiefs who had been to call on President Harrison thus characterized him:

Said Young Man Afraid of his Horses: "He is a man of the old trail; he will never make a new one!"

White Ghost said: "There is strong religious principle in him."

Then American Horse spoke up. "The missionaries tell us that a man cannot have two masters; then how can he be a religious man and a politician at the same time?"

An old chief said of President McKinley: "I never knew a white man show so much love for mother and wife." "He has a bigger heart than most white men," declared Littlefish, "and this is unfortunate for him. The white man is a man of business, and has no use for a heart."

One day, I found a number of the chiefs in the Senate gallery. They observed closely the faces and bearing of the legislators and then gave their verdict. One man they compared to a fish. Another had not the attitude of a true man; that is, he held to a pose. Senator Morgan of Alabama they called a great councillor. Senator Hoar they estimated as a patriotic and just statesman. They picked out Senator Platt of Connecticut as being very cautious and a diplomat. They had much difficulty in judging Senator Tillman, but on the whole they considered him to be a fighting man, governed by his emotions rather than his judgment. Some said, he is a loyal friend; others held the reverse. Senator Turpie of Indiana they took for a preacher, and were pleased with his air of godliness and reverence. Senator Frye of

Maine they thought must be a rarity among white men—honest to the core!

It was John Grass who declared that Grover Cleveland was the bravest white chief he had ever known. "The harder you press him," said he, "the stronger he stands."

Theodore Roosevelt has been well known to the Sioux for over twenty-five years, dating from the years of his ranch life. He was well liked by them as a rule. Spotted Horse said of him, "While he talked, I forgot that he was a white man."

During Mr. Roosevelt's second administration, there was much disappointment among the Indians. They had cherished hopes of an honest deal, but things seemed to be worse than ever. There were more frauds committed; and in the way of legislation, the Burke bill was distinctly a backward step. The Dawes bill was framed in the interest of the Indians; the Burke bill was for the grafters. Therefore there was much discouragement.

I have been much interested in the point of view of these older Indians. Our younger element has now been so thoroughly drilled in the motives and methods of the white man, at the same time losing the old mother and family training through being placed in boarding schools from six years of age onward, that they have really become an entirely different race.

During this phase of my life, I was brought face to face with a new phase of progress among my people of the Dakotas. Several of their reservations were allotted in severalty and the Indians became full citizens and voters. As the population of these new states was still small and scattered, the new voters, although few in number, were of distinct interest to the candidates for office, and their favor was eagerly sought. In some counties, the Indian vote held the balance of power. Naturally, they looked to the best educated men of their race to explain to them the principles and platforms of the political parties.

At first they continued to get together according to old custom, calling a council and giving a preliminary feast, at which two or three steers would be killed for a barbecue. After dinner, the tribal herald called the men together to hear the candidate or his representative. I took active part in one or two campaigns;

but they have now a number of able young men who expound politics to them locally.

Some persons imagine that we are still wild savages, living on the hunt or on rations; but as a matter of fact, we Sioux are now fully entrenched, for all practical purposes, in the warfare of civilized life.

XI. Back to the Woods

In the summer of 1910, I accepted a commission to search out and purchase rare curios and ethnological specimens for one of the most important collections in the country. Very few genuine antiques are now to be found among Indians living on reservations, and the wilder and more scattered bands who still treasure them cannot easily be induced to give them up. My method was one of indirection. I would visit for several days in a camp where I knew, or had reason to believe, that some of the coveted articles were to be found. After I had talked much with the leading men, feasted them, and made them presents, a slight hint would often result in the chief or medicine man "presenting" me with some object of historic or ceremonial interest, which etiquette would not permit to be "sold," and which a white man would probably not have been allowed to see at all.

Within the zone of railroads and automobiles there is, I believe, only one region left in which a few roving bands of North American Indians still hold civilization at bay. The great inland seas of northern Minnesota and the Province of Ontario are surrounded by almost impenetrable jungle, the immense bogs called "muskeggs" filled with tamaracks, and the higher land with Norway, white and "jack" pines, white and red cedar, poplar and birch. The land is a paradise for moose, deer and bears, as well as the smaller fur-bearers, and the glistening black waters are a congenial home for northern fish of all kinds, of which the sturgeon is king. The waterfowl breed there in countless numbers. There are blueberries and cranberries in abundance, while the staple cereal of that region, the full-flavored wild rice, is found in the inland bays by thousand of acres.

Of this miniature world of freedom and plenty a few northern Ojibways, a branch of the great Algonquin race, are the present inhabitants, living quite to themselves and almost unconscious of the bare pathos of their survival. Here the early French traders reaped their harvest, and for a century and a half the land was under the despotic rule of the Hudson Bay Company. A powerful forerunner of civilization, this company never civilized the natives, who, moreover, had heard the "Black Robe" priests say their masses under the solemn shade of the Norway pines upon their island homes, long before Lewis and Clark crossed the continent, and before many of the prairie tribes had so much as looked upon the face of the white man. Fortunately or unfortunately, the labyrinth in which they dwell has thus far protected them far more effectually than any treaty rights could possibly do from his almost indecent enterprise.

I know of no Indians within the borders of the United States, except those of Leech, Cass and Red Lakes in Minnesota, who still sustain themselves after the old fashion by hunting, fishing and the gathering of wild rice and berries. They do, to be sure, have a trifle of annuity money from the sale of their pine lands, and now and then they sell a few trinkets. Their permanent houses are of logs or frame, but they really do not live in them except during the coldest part of the year. Even then, some of them may be found far away from their villages, trapping for furs, which may still be disposed of at convenient points along the Canadian border. They travel by canoe or on foot, as they own very few horses, and there are no roads through the forest—only narrow trails, deeply grooved in the virgin soil.

The Leech Lake Ojibways, to whom I made my first visit, appear perfectly contented and irresponsible. They have plenty to eat of the choicest wild game, wild rice and berries. The making of maple sugar is a leading industry. The largest band and by far the most interesting is that which inhabits Bear Island, plants no gardens, will have nothing to do with schools or churches, and meets annually, as of old, for the "Grand Medicine Dance," or sacred festival, invoking the protection and blessing of the "Great Mystery" for the year to come.

I am a Sioux, and the Ojibways were once the fiercest of our enemies, yet I was kindly welcomed by the principal chief, Majigabo, who even permitted me to witness the old rites upon their "sacred ground." This particular spot, they told me, had been in use for more than forty years, and the moose-hide drum, stretched upon a cylinder of bass-wood, was fully as venerable. The dance-hall was about a hundred feet long, roofed with poles and thatch. In the center was a rude altar, and the entrance faced the rising sun. While the ceremonies went on, groups of young men were sitting in the shade and gambling with primitive dice—small carved bones shaken in a polished bowl of bird's-eye maple.

Majigabo is one of the few Indians left alive who has ventured to defy a great government with a handful of savages. Only a few years ago, Captain Wilkinson was shot down at the head of his troop, while advancing to frighten the Bear Islanders into obedience. The trouble originated in the illegal sale of whisky to the Indians. One of the tribesmen was summoned to Duluth as a witness, and at the close of the trial turned loose to walk home, a distance of over a hundred miles. The weather was severe and he reached his people half-starved and sick from exposure, and the next time one was summoned, he not unnaturally refused to appear. After the death of Captain Wilkinson, no further attempt was made at coercion.

"They can take everything else, but they must let me and these island people alone," the chief said to me, and I could not but sympathize with his attitude. Only last spring he refused to allow the census taker to enumerate his people.

The next man I went to see was Boggimogishig. The old war chief of the Sugar Point band was one of those who most frequently went against the Eastern Sioux, and was often successful. This good fortune was attributed largely to the influence of the sacred war club, which had been handed down through several generations of dauntless leaders. I made use of the old-time Indian etiquette, as well as of all the wit and humor at my command, to win a welcome, and finally obtained from the old man the history and traditions of his people, so far as he knew them, and even the famous war club itself!

At Red Lake, I found the men just returned from a successful moose hunt, and although they greeted me kindly, it appeared that some of the older warriors, recalling hand-to-hand scrimmages with my forbears, were somewhat embarrassed by the presence of a Sioux visitor. However, after I had been properly introduced, and had conformed with the good old customs relating to intertribal meetings, I secured several things that I had come in search of, and among them some very old stories. It appears that a battle was once fought between Ojibways and Sioux near the mouth of the stream called Battle Creek, and while the waters of the stream ran with blood, the color was even discernible upon the shores of the lake, which has ever since been known as Red Lake. It was this battle, indeed, which finally decided the question of occupancy, for it is said that although my people succeeded for the time in holding off the Ojibways, and cast many of the bodies of their dead enemies into the river, they lost so heavily themselves and became so disheartened that they then left forever behind them their forest life and exchanged the canoe and birch-bark teepee for the prairie and the buffalo.

But it is on Rainy Lake, remote and solitary, and still further to the north and west upon the equally lovely Lake of the Woods, that I found the true virgin wilderness, the final refuge, as it appears, of American big game and primitive man. The international line at this point is formed by the Rainy River, lying deep in its rocky bed and connecting the two lakes, both of which are adorned with thousands of exquisite islands of a gem-like freshness and beauty. The clear, black waters have washed, ground and polished these rocky islets into every imaginable fantastic shape and they are all carpeted with velvety mosses in every shade of gray and green, and canopied with fairy-like verdure. In every direction one is beckoned by vistas of extraordinary charm.

These aboriginal woodsmen are in type quite distinct from the Plains Indians. They are generally tall and well-proportioned, of somewhat lighter complexion than their brethren to the southward, and very grave and reticent. Their homes and food are practically those of two centuries ago, the only change observable being that the inconvenient blanket is for the most part discarded and the men carry guns instead of bows and arrows.

It was the middle of August, the time for tying into bundles the wild rice straw, in the great bays where nature has so plentifully sown it. To each family belong its sheaves, and when the tying is finished, they are apt to linger in the neighborhood, the women making sacks while the men hunt. A month later comes the harvest. Two by two they go out in canoes, one to paddle, while the other seizes the bundle of rice straw and strikes a few smart blows with a stick. The ripe grain rattles into the canoe, which, when half full, is emptied on shore, and so on until the watery fields are cleared.

I had now to follow these family groups to their hidden resorts, and the sweet roving instinct of the wild took forcible hold upon me once more. I was eager to realize for a few perfect days the old, wild life as I knew it in my boyhood, and I set out with an Ojibway guide in his birch canoe, taking with me little that belonged to the white man, except his guns, fishing tackle, knives, and tobacco. The guide carried some Indian-made maple sugar and a sack of wild rice, a packet of black tea and a kettle, and we had a blanket apiece. Only think of pitching your tent upon a new island every day in the year! Upon many a little rocky terrace, shaded by pine and cedar trees, hard by a tiny harbor with its fleet of birchen canoes, the frail bark lodges stood about in groups, looking as if they had grown there. Before each lodge there is a fireplace, and near at hand the women of the family may often be seen making nets and baskets, or cooking the simple meal.

Early in the summer mornings there is a pleasant stir in camp, when they glide in canoes over the placid waters, lifting their nets full of glistening fish. Perhaps the sturgeon net is successful; then laughter and whoops of excitement break the stillness, for the king of the lake fights for his life and pulls the boat about vigorously before he is finally knocked on the head and towed into camp.

Up on Seine Bay the favorite sport was hunting the loon, which scarcely ever takes to the wing, but dives on being approached. Most people would be put to it to guess in which

WITH GUIDE AND BARK CANOE, ON RAINY LAKE, ONTARIO.

direction he would reappear, at a distance of from a quarter to half a mile, but these sons of nature have learned his secret. As soon as he goes under, the canoes race for a certain point, and invariably the bird comes up among them. He is greeted with derisive laughter and cheers and immediately dives again, and the maneuver is repeated until he is winded and caught. The flesh of the loon has a strong, fishy flavor, but these Indians are very fond of it. With them nothing goes to waste; all meat or fish not needed for immediate use is cut into thin strips and smoked or dried; the hoofs of deer and moose are made into trinkets, the horns into spoons or tobacco boards, and the bones pounded to boil out the fat, which is preserved in dried bladders or bags of pelican skin.

At North Bay I heard of a remarkable old woman, said to be well over ninety years of age, the daughter of a long-time chief during the good old days. I called at her solitary birch-bark teepee, and found her out, but she soon returned bent under a load of bark for making mats, with roots and willow twigs for dye. She was persuaded to sit for her picture and even to tell some old stories of her people, which she did with much vivacity. There are less than a hundred of them left!

The name given to this ancient crone by the lumber-jacks is shockingly irreverent. It is told that when she was a handsome young woman, her father the ruling chief and honored by the Hudson Bay Company, more than one of its employees came courting after the fashion of those days. But the daughter of the woods could not endure the sight of a white man, with his repulsive hairy face. It seems that one day, when she was approached by a bearded voyageur, she screamed and raised her knife, so that the man fled, cursing her. Thereafter, whenever she saw a white man, she would innocently repeat his oath, until she came to be known among them by that name.

As we wound in and out of the island labyrinth, new beauties met us at every turn. At one time there were not less than eight moose in sight, and the deer were plentiful and fearless. As we glided through the water, the Ojibway repeated in his broken dialect some of their traditions. We passed "Massacre island," where, more than a hundred years ago, some French traders are

said to have brought the "fire water" to a large village of innocent natives, thinking thus to buy their furs for a trifle. But the
Indians, when crazed with liquor, rose up and killed them all
instead, even a Catholic priest who was unfortunately of the
party. Since that day, the spirit of the "Black Robe," who died
praying, is believed to haunt the deserted island, and no Indian
ever sets foot there.

Every day it became harder for me to leave the woods. Finally
I took passage on a gasoline launch that plied between a lumber
camp and the little city of International Falls. The air had been
dense with smoke all day because of immense forest fires on
both sides of the lake. As it grew dark we entered a narrow chan-
nel between the islands, when the wind suddenly rose, and the
pilot feared lest we should be blown from the only known
course, for much of the lake is not charted. He swung about for
the nearest islands, a cluster of three, knowing that only on one
side of one of these was it possible to land. It was dark as pitch
and raining hard when we were struck broad side on by a heavy
wave; the windows were knocked out and all the lights extin-
guished.

There was nothing to do but jump and swim for it, and it
seems almost a miracle that we all landed safely. There were just
four of us playing Robinson Crusoe on a lovely little isle of about
an acre in extent—too small to harbor any game. The boat was
gone with all its freight, except a few things that drifted ashore.
Here we remained for two nights and a day before we were discovered.

This accident delayed me a day or two, as I had to buy another canoe and provisions for my last plunge into the wilderness. It carried me up Seine Bay and into the Seine River. One
day we came unexpectedly upon a little Indian village of neatly
made bark houses in a perfect state of preservation, but to my
surprise it was uninhabited. What was still stranger, I found that
whoever lived there had left all their goods behind, dishes,
clothing, even bundles of furs all moth-eaten and ruined. We
reached there late in the afternoon, and I immediately decided
to stay the night. After supper, the guide told me that a band of
Indians had lived here every winter for several years, hunting

for the Hudson Bay Company. One winter many of their children were attacked by a disease unknown to them, and after several had died, the people fled in terror, leaving everything behind them. This happened, he said, eleven years before. While he was talking, beside the fire we had built in the rude mud chimney of one of the deserted cabins, in the perfectly still night, it all seemed weird and mysterious. Suddenly we heard a loud scratching on the bark door, as if some hand were feeling for the latch. He stopped speaking and we looked at one another. The scratching was repeated. "Shall I open the door?" I said. I had my hand on the trigger of my Smith and Wesson. He put more sticks on the fire. When I got the door open, there stood the biggest turtle I have ever seen, raised upon his hind feet, his eyes shining, his tail defiantly lifted, as if to tell us that he was at home there and we were the intruders.

XII. The Soul of the White Man

M y last work under the auspices of the Government was the revision of the Sioux allotment rolls, including the determination of family groups, and the assignment of surnames when these were lacking. Originally, the Indians had no family names, and confusion has been worse confounded by the admission to the official rolls of vulgar nicknames, incorrect translations, and English cognomens injudiciously bestowed upon children in the various schools. Mr. Hamlin Garland and Dr. George Bird Grinnell interested themselves in this matter some years ago, and President Roosevelt foresaw the difficulties and complications in the way of land inheritance, hence my unique commission.

My method was to select from the personal names of a family, one which should be reasonably short, euphonious, and easily pronounced by the white man in the vernacular; or, failing this, a short translation in which the essential meaning should be preserved. All the brothers, their wives and children were then grouped under this as a family name, provided their consent could be obtained to the arrangement.

While fully appreciating the Indian's viewpoint, I have tried to convince him of the sincerity of his white friends, and that conflicts between the two races have been due as much to mutual misunderstandings as to the selfish greed of the white man. These children of nature once had faith in man as well as in God. To-day, they would suspect even their best friend. A "century of dishonor" and abuse of their trust has brought them to this. Accordingly, it was rumored among them that the revision of names was another cunning scheme of the white man to defraud them of the little land still left in their possession. The older men would sit in my office and watch my work day after day, before being convinced that the undertaking was really intended for their benefit and that of their heirs. Once satisfied, they were of great assistance, for some of them knew by heart the family tree of nearly every Indian in that particular band for four generations. Their memories are remarkable, and many a fact of historic interest came up in the course of our discussions.

Such names as "Young Man of whose Horses the Enemy is Afraid," "He Kills them on Horseback," and the like, while highly regarded among us, are not easily rendered into English nor pronounced in the Dakota, and aside from such troubles, I had many difficulties with questionable marriages and orphaned children whose ancestry was not clear. Then there were cases of Indian women who had married Unites States soldiers and the children had been taken away from the tribe in infancy, but later returned as young men and women to claim their rights in the tribal lands.

I was directed not to recognize a plurality of wives, such as still existed among a few of the older men. Old White Bull was a fine example of the old type, and I well remember his answer when I reluctantly informed him that each man must choose one wife who should bear his name. "What!" he exclaimed, "these two women are sisters, both of whom have been my wives for over half a century. I know the way of the white man; he takes women unknown to each other and to his law. These two have been faithful to me and I have been faithful to them. Their children are my children and their grandchildren are mine. We are now living together as brother and sisters. All the people know that we have been happy together, and nothing but death can separate us."

This work occupied me for six years, and gave me insight into the relationships and intimate history of thirty thousand Sioux.

My first book, "Indian Boyhood," embodying the recollections of my wild life, appeared in 1902, and the favor with which it was received has encouraged me to attempt a fuller expression of our people's life from the inside. The present is the eighth that I have done, always with the devoted cooperation of my wife. Although but one book, "Wigwam Evenings," bears both our names, we have worked together, she in the little leisure remaining to the mother of six children, and I in the intervals of lecturing and other employment. For the past twelve years our home has been in a New England college town, and our greatest personal concern the upbringing and education of our children.

None of my earlier friends who knew me well would ever have believed that I was destined to appear in the rôle of a public speaker! It may be that I shared the native gift of oratory in some degree, but I had also the Indian reticence with strangers. Perhaps the one man most responsible for this phase of my work, aside from circumstances, was Major James B. Pond of New York City, the famous lyceum manager. Soon after the publication of "Indian Boyhood," I came from South Dakota to Brooklyn by invitation of the Twentieth Century Club of that city, to address them on the Indian. Major Pond heard of this and invited me to luncheon. He had my book with him, and after a good deal of talk, he persuaded me to go on the lecture platform under his management. He took the most cordial interest in the matter, and himself prepared the copy for my first circular. His untimely death during the next summer put a damper upon my beginning; nevertheless I filled all the dates he had made for me, and finding a growing demand, I have continued in the field ever since.

My chief object has been, not to entertain, but to present the American Indian in his true character before Americans. The barbarous and atrocious character commonly attributed to him has dated from the transition period, when the strong drink, powerful temptations, and commercialism of the white man led to deep demoralization. Really it was a campaign of education on the Indian and his true place in American history.

I have been, on the whole, happily surprised to meet with so cordial a response. Again and again I have been told by recognized thinkers, "You present an entirely new viewpoint. We can never again think of the Indian as we have done before." A great psychologist wrote me after reading "The Soul of the Indian":

"My God! why did we not know these things sooner?" Many of my hearers have admitted that morality and spirituality are found to thrive better under the simplest conditions than in a highly organized society, and that the virtues are more readily cultivated where the "struggle for existence" is merely a struggle with the forces of nature, and not with one's fellow-men.

The philosophy of the original American was demonstrably on a high plane, his gift of eloquence, wit, humor and poetry is well established; his democracy and community life was much nearer the ideal than ours to-day; his standard of honor and friendship unsurpassed, and all his faults are the faults of generous youth.

It was not until I felt that I had to a degree established these claims, that I consented to appear on the platform in our ancestral garb of honor. I feel that I was a pioneer in this new line of defense of the native American, not so much of his rights in the land as of his character and religion. I am glad that the drift is now toward a better understanding, and that he is become the acknowledged hero of the Boy Scouts and Camp Fire Girls, as well as of many artists, sculptors, and sincere writers.

I was invited to represent the North American Indian at the First Universal Races Congress in London, England, in 1911. It was a great privilege to attend that gathering of distinguished representatives of 53 different nationalities, come together to mutually acquaint themselves with one another's progress and racial ideals. I was entertained by some well known men, but there was little time for purely social enjoyment. What impressed me most was the perfect equality of the races, which formed the background of all the discussions. It was declared at the outset that there is no superior race, and no inferior, since individuals of all races have proved their innate capacity by their standing in the universities of the world, and it has not seldom happened that men of the undeveloped races have surpassed students of the most advanced races in scholarship and ability.

One little incident caused some of the delegates of the Asiatic peoples to approach me with a special friendliness. I was at a committee meeting where the platform of the Congress was being drafted, and as the first paragraph was read, I noticed that the word "Christian" appeared several times. I rose and said, "While I am myself a believer in the simple principles of Christianity, we who are met here are not all of that religion, and I would suggest that we substitute a term to which we can all subscribe, since we meet here not in the name, but in the spirit of Christianity, of universal brotherhood." Several sprang up to second the motion, among them Mr. John Milholland and Dr. Felix Adler, and as I saw Mr. Edwin D. Mead of Boston near by, I began to feel more at home. I was invited by some oriental representatives present to visit them in their own country, but as I was tied up with Chautauqua engagements, I had to take the next boat for home.

A very pleasant occasion of my meeting men and women distinguished in literature, was the banquet given to Mark Twain on his seventieth birthday. Another interesting meeting was the dinner given by the Rocky Mountain Club of New York to fifteen western governors. I believe I was the only speaker there who was not a governor! When I addressed the Camp Fire Club of America, composed largely of big game hunters in all parts of the world, I began by telling them that I had slept with a grizzly bear for three months, and often eaten with him, but had never thought of giving him away. They seemed to enter into my mood; and when I went on to tell the old chief's story of the beaver woman with one hand (she had lost the other in a steel trap) and what she and her descendants did for the tribes of men and animals, as compared with the harm wrought by the too hasty builders of a frontier town, I could not ask for a more sympathetic audience.

It has been my privilege to visit nearly all sections of our country on lecture tours, including semi-tropical Florida and the Pacific coast, the great prairie states, and almost every nook and corner of picturesque New England. I have been entertained at most of our great colleges and universities, from coast to coast, and had the honor of acquaintance with many famous and interesting people, among whom I might name almost at random, W. D. Howells, Hamlin Garland, Ernest Thompson Seton, Dr. George Bird Grinnell, authors; Lorado Taft, sculptor (at the unveiling of whose colossal Black Hawk I was privileged to officiate), Edwin W. Deming, Ernest Blumenschein, and other noted artists; Mme. Bloomfield Zeisler, pianist; John Hays Hammond, engineer; Presidents G. Stanley Hall, Ernest Fox Nichols, Eliot, Stryker, Harry Pratt Judson, Dr. Luther Gulick, and other noted educators; Rabbi Stephen S. Wise, several bishops, and prominent clergymen of all denominations, together with a large circle not so well known to the public, but whose society has been to me equally stimulating and delightful.

Like every one else who is more or less in the public eye, I have a large correspondence from unknown friends, and among the most inspiring letters received have been those from foreign countries, where, until the outbreak of the European war, I had not only generous critics, but translators of my books in France, Germany, Austria, Bohemia, Denmark. I am frequently asked to recommend to readers books on all phases of Indian life and art, also to criticize such books both in print and in manuscript.

My work for the Boy Scouts, whose program appeals to me strongly, has given me a good deal of practice in camp management, finally leading to the organization of summer camps for both boys and girls on charming Granite Lake in the hills of southern New Hampshire, where my whole family are enthusiastic helpers in the development of this form of open-air education, patterned largely upon my own early training.

From the time I first accepted the Christ ideal it has grown upon me steadily, but I also see more and more plainly our modern divergence from that ideal. I confess I have wondered much that Christianity is not practised by the very people who vouch for that wonderful conception of exemplary living. It appears that they are anxious to pass on their religion to all races of men, but keep very little of it themselves. I have not yet seen the meek inherit the earth, or the peacemakers receive high honor.

Why do we find so much evil and wickedness practised by the nations composed of professedly "Christian" individuals? The pages of history are full of licensed murder and the plundering of weaker and less developed peoples, and obviously the world to-day has not outgrown this system. Behind the material and intellectual splendor of our civilization, primitive savagery and cruelty and lust hold sway, undiminished, and as it seems, unheeded. When I let go of my simple, instinctive nature religion, I hoped to gain something far loftier as well as more satisfying to the reason. Alas! it is also more confusing and contradictory. The higher and spiritual life, though first in theory, is clearly secondary, if not entirely neglected, in actual practice. When I reduce civilization to its lowest terms, it becomes a system of life based upon trade. The dollar is the measure of value, and *might* still spells *right;* otherwise, why war?

Yet even in deep jungles God's own sunlight penetrates, and I stand before my own people still as an advocate of civilization. Why? First, because there is no chance for our former simple life any more; and second, because I realize that the white man's religion is not responsible for his mistakes. There is every evidence that God has given him all the light necessary by which to live in peace and good-will with his brother; and we also know that many brilliant civilizations have collapsed in physical and moral decadence. It is for us to avoid their fate if we can.

I am an Indian; and while I have learned much from civilization, for which I am grateful, I have never lost my Indian sense of right and justice. I am for development and progress along social and spiritual lines, rather than those of commerce, nationalism, or material efficiency. Nevertheless, so long as I live, I am an American.

THE END

Index